ESSAYS ON ART AND ONTOLOGY

ESSAYS ON ART

AND

ONTOLOGY

LEONE VIVANTE

Translated from the Italian by Arturo Vivante
Foreword by Brewster Ghiselin

University of Utah Press
Salt Lake City
1980

The translator wishes to acknowledge the kind permission of the following journals to reprint these essays in translation:

Revista de Filosofia for "Quattro tipi di teorie d'estetica" (Vol. XLVIII, April 1957); "Il nuovo ontologico e la positività dell'essere" (Vol. XLIX, Oct. 1958); "La corporeità immediata del pensiero" (Vol. LI, April 1960); "Difficoltà del concetto dell'inderivato attivo" (Vol. LII, April 1961); "L'infinito soggettivo e l'indiviso" (Vol. LIII, Jan. 1962).

Realismo Lirico for "Il nuovo ontologico e l'arte" (No. 70–71, 1965).

The Southern Journal of Philosophy, which published earlier versions of Chapter 6 (Winter 1966) and Chapter 7 (Summer 1968).

I Problemi della Pedagogia for "Il principio dell'indeterminazione e l'infinito soggettivo" (No. 5–6, Sept.–Dec. 1969).

LIBRARY OF CONGRESS CATALOGUING IN PUBLICATION DATA

Vivante, Leone, 1887–
    Essays on art and ontology.

"These essays were published separately . . . and are
collected and translated here for the first time."
    1. Ontology — Collected works. 2. Aesthetics —
Collected works. I. Title.
B3656.V52E5   1980   111   79-89879
ISBN 0-87480-100-1

Contents

Other Books by Leone Vivante

1920 *Principii de etica.* Rome: Maglione e Strini.

1922 *Della intelligenza nell'espressione.* Rome: Maglione e Strini.

1925 *Note sopra la originalità del pensiero.* Rome: Maglione e Strini.

Intelligence in Expression. Translated by Professor Brodrick-Bullock, with a foreword by H. Wildon Carr. London: The C. W. Daniel Company.

1927 *Notes on the Originality of Thought.* Translated by Professor Brodrick-Bullock. London: John Lane, The Bodley Head.

1935 *Grazia e arbitrio.* Rome: Novissima.

1937 *Studi sulle precognizioni.* Florence: Vallecchi editore.

1938 *Il concetto dell'indeterminazione.* Florence: Vallecchi editore.

1939 *Indétermination et création.* Translated by Lorenzo Ercole Lanza. Paris: F. Sorlot.

1947 *La poesia inglese ed il suo contributo alla conoscenza dello spirito.* Florence: Vallecchi editore.

1950 *English Poetry and Its Contribution to the Knowledge of a Creative Principle.* With a preface by T. S. Eliot. London: Faber and Faber; New York: Macmillan. American edition: Carbondale, Ill.: Southern Illinois University Press, 1963.

1953 *Elementi di una filosofia della potenzialità.* Florence: Vallecchi editore.

1955 *A Philosophy of Potentiality.* London: Routledge & Kegan Paul.

Acknowledgments

I wish to thank Trudy McMurrin, who edited this book with such admirable skill and understanding; Brewster Ghiselin for his invaluable suggestions and revisions, and for his help and encouragement at all times. Indeed, without the aid that his vision as a poet and profound interest in the creative process lent it, this book could hardly have been brought to light. I would also like to thank Nancy Vivante, Paolo Vivante, and R. W. Flint for their considerable assistance in the translation.

Arturo Vivante

Leone Vivante

Leone Vivante was born in Parma in 1887. He was the son of Cesare Vivante, an authority on Italian jurisprudence, and his mother was Lia Ascoli, daughter of the great philologist Graziadio Isaia Ascoli.

After graduating in law at the University of Rome, he served as an infantry officer in World War I; in 1920 he married the painter Elena de Bosis, daughter of Adolfo de Bosis, poet and translator of Shelley. They had three sons, Paolo, Arturo, and Cesare, and one daughter, Charis.

Vivante soon turned from legal theory to philosophy, publishing in the twenties a series of works on ethics and the theory of knowledge, in which he expounded the existence of an imaginative creative principle at work in art and moral activity, as well as in ordinary perception. In the thirties came his studies on precognition and his book on the concept of indeterminism; these developed the belief in a spontaneous force active in nature while elaborating on the issues of creativity and predetermined necessity. Such interest in a creative principle naturally led Vivante to the field of aesthetics — most notably in his best-known book, that on English poetry, which he wrote in the early forties in England, where he had repaired with his family as a refugee from fascism.

It will be seen that Vivante was far removed from the prevailing philosophical trends of the age — from such an analytical approach as that of the positivists, from the negations of existentialism. He was thus a solitary thinker and had no close friends among philosophers, with some notable exceptions such as Bosanquet and Santayana. He found greater affinity in such poets and critics as Herbert Read, Brewster Ghiselin, and John H. Muirhead. T. S. Eliot, who wrote the preface to *English Poetry,* is said to have changed his view of Shelley under Vivante's influence.

This may explain the fact that Vivante never sought any academic position and stayed away from universities except for lecture tours in the United States and England. He mostly lived in the country at the Villa Solaia near Siena, where he returned after the war and grew an orchard of fruit trees. He died there in 1970.

Paolo Vivante

Foreword

For more than forty years the work of Leone Vivante has held
the attention and respect of a few of the foremost among his con-
temporaries. Several of these have written of it with discernment
and deep appreciation, among them T. S. Eliot and Camillo
Sbarbaro. Yet despite its powerful and sensitive treatment of some
of the most challenging problems of philosophy — particularly in
epistemology and aesthetics — Leone Vivante's work has never
been so generally acclaimed as it deserved to be. So long ago as the
mid-thirties, when he had already published three notable books,
this neglect was deplored by the distinguished Italian critic Alfredo
Gargiulo. And twenty and thirty years later, the effect of long con-
tinuance of neglect was evident in the quiet serenity with which
Vivante voiced his thought, whether in public lectures or in conversation: blithely and uninsistently, like a bird alone with his song
in a forest where there might or might not be anyone besides himself to hear it.

Central to all of Leone Vivante's philosophical insight is the
intuition of subjective life in its immediate force and character, as
directly known, appreciated, and understood in its whole rich

presentation, psychic energy ceaselessly active, not as something merely conditioned, a stream of impressions and responses compelled and endured, but as exigent being, spontaneously evocative, formative, autonomous in movement, the primary fact of experience. That intuition is the basis from which the thrust of his thinking arises, and the support upon which every demonstration comes to rest in renewed conviction. The changing trends and purposes of his discourse sooner or later return his thought to it, but always with a different emphasis, as the advance of a dancer returns the foot to its ground of vantage.

Vivante writes as a philosopher expert and rigorous in exposition and exegesis, but also, in the culminations of his argument, as a poet: that is, he is concerned for the full body of insight alive in all the modes of sentience. So for instance in writing of an inexhaustible "implication of values inherent in the concept of true positivity" — perpetually originative power — in subjective life, Vivante subtitles his discussion "The Rose of Values" — "La Rosa dei Valori." And in that title, by means of the word denoting the living flower that is of all flowers most exalted and the most compelling and universal emblem, and by the very form of the phrase suggesting also the rose or flower of the winds, *rosa dei venti*, figure of the compass card — instrument of orientation, he fuses with concrete imagery, undepleted of associations, ideas of vital unity and centrality and of the whole range of those ends toward which mankind may look and move.

His intent in exposition is not, finally, to structure an intellectual perspective upon an object — or a universe — exhaustively determined in a nexus of propositions. His arguments are designed to show the way: through clearing the path of obstacles imposed by ignorance, common illusion, unsound reasoning, to lead the reader to that same intuitive appreciation of the inmost elemental life which he took to be the source of understanding, the ground of delight. By a myriad of devices, by minute, exhaustive examinations of various modes of thinking, and of arguments from premise to conclusion, by suggestion and asseveration, he will urge and lead us through every bog and barren and labyrinth and garden of delusion to the verge of light. But there we are to be left, with silence in our ears, and with eyes open. His aim is — ultimately — not to tell us something, but to give access.

Pazienza: patience. If his whole drift is not at once apparent, that may be because it must carry a long, arduous way, to a state of mind, a mode of understanding and of seeing — a vision — that is not determined by intellectual considerations alone yet must be made more truly secure through submitting attention to them. If we think we have already attained that security, independently, we may find our conviction confirmed afresh by Leone Vivante's expositions. Their strict revelations will combine in one perspective, like a wide landscape strongly lighted.

It was clearly Vivante's understanding that by looking beyond the ego to what authorizes its growth and sustains its integrity we can free ourselves from submission to those of its demands which entrammel and constrict because they issue from a limited construct that accords too little with the whole need of our nature. The ego, that largely benign psychic structure which assists in maintaining the synthesis of subjective life, does not — as we know — comprise the whole of it. The popular notion of that whole — and by and large the current scientific conception of it — provides an image or hypothesis of an invisible supplement of the ego and its sphere: a spiritual limbo astir with unconscious or subconscious contents and urgencies, helpful or hindering. I can think of nothing further from Leone Vivante's understanding than this olla podrida aboil on the fires of speculation. In envisaging the scope and evocative force of the psyche in its wholeness, Vivante looks to nothing so predetermined and mechanical in its action as that thin-crusted slightly sulphurous black pool.

He proposes that all human beings take notice of their own most immediate experience, and found and shape their understanding upon that. Turning attention to the momentary aspects of subjective life, Vivante is determined to see, and to help his readers to see, what goes forward at the quick and instant of its happening, as the delimiting forms characteristic of human sentience, each charged with energy and meaning, emerge and change and fade away. In the context of these transformations, when they are truly autonomous, not merely stereotypes of behavior contravening need, he discerns an accompaniment not commonly noticed or considered: an awareness intense and wide but formless, intuition of an infinite inward urgency qualified by no specific determination and yet by its own featureless imperative calling into being the unique psychic energies, forms, and meanings constitutive of the substance and order of insights and actions.

The forms serving that fulfillment in delineating its order may be new-made in the instant of realization. Or they may be drawn from the resources of culture. But in either case the force and the purport thus ordered must originate in the active subject: they cannot be infused by another. As Vivante has explained in his book *Elementi di una filosofia della potenzialità,* "There is in the spirit an intrinsic power, to which we must refer. Ultimately nothing great, nothing truly vital, is transmitted!" For the formed figures of realization, even those preshaped by other minds and hands — as if ready-made — can be truly known only as some user gives to them (configurations otherwise inert) the force and scope of his own energies, his own transfiguring spirit in action. To possess them at all he must breathe into them individual life. But in doing so, he makes them immediately new. They glow and vibrate then with fresh being, and with the infinite promise of awakened power. As Vivante remarks in a later context, "An atom of creation changes the face of the world . . . ."

Eased of its grips and trammels, moving at large in immediate being, in fulfillment instantly complete, life enacting all its need is bonded only in delight. It is in that mode of realization, Vivante believed, that we discover the true contrary of the coarctative forces of the ego. And — with due allowance for the limitations of terms — of the superego also. Thus Vivante appears to ally himself less with Freud than with Jung. Yet he is independent of both in his thinking, most notably so in his skeptical view of the notion of structured determinants acting in a somehow subconscious sphere of the psyche.

The sense of amplitude and of uncommitted freedom that envelops and transfigures every particular of the most vital awareness is not rare in human experience. But it is without shape, evanescent, and elusive. It cannot be seized on and detained for examination and report. Often, perhaps, it may be noticed only in its effect on the sensibilities, as a mood, as some fleeting, hardly explicable happiness or seemingly causeless exultation or joy.

The ground of indeterminate awareness cannot be surveyed and set forth plotted and circumscribed in the restrictive focus of attention. For not even those particulars of substance and structure that it has evoked and sustained can adumbrate it. The merest vague notions of things or the most rarefied abstractions of thought put forward to represent it will focus their own specific illumination, and displace that other as if it were darkness. Concepts, in portraying it, show us their own features. Names mask it.

It has all too frequently, therefore, been discounted in theory, as illusion, or groundless feeling, or emotional overtone, or as sensation. Or it has been given religious import dogmatically hedged. Vivante's first concern is to attend to it, to know it as it is in itself, and to consider its occasions and connections, then to test, to demonstrate, to illustrate, to exemplify, and so to share his insight.

He considered that work of patient attention, exploration, and exposition the main burden of his calling as philosopher, and his responsibility as a man. This last of his books has been posthumously translated from essays that appeared in Italian journals, except for two that were published in America during his lifetime. Not long before he died, he gave the essays a tentative order. The book can speak for him, the final formulation of his quintessential insight, as he wished.

Brewster Ghiselin

ESSAYS ON ART AND ONTOLOGY

CHAPTER 1

Four Types of Aesthetic Theory

Aesthetic theories may be divided into four groups: (1) theories of imitation, (2) pragmatic theories, (3) physiological theories, and (4) theories of expression as original reality.

1. THEORIES OF IMITATION. The theories and tendencies with which I am here concerned could be called by other names, such as 'naturalism,' 'naive objective realism,' 'literal transcription,' or 'duplication of objective reality'; or also, with different overtones, 'illusionism.'

According to these theories, the true value of a work of art consists in its convincing representation of a given object. Such a standard is altogether inadequate: imitation implies above all a labor of external construction, skill, and technique, and these are no justification for what is commonly held to be value in art. Judging by their respective achievements, it is clear that the artist can seldom compete with the scientist in minute observation; and, as everyone knows, he is even less the rival of the photographer.

Nevertheless this is a commonly held view; in the past we have seen it affirmed by great artists and writers. Here are some of the reasons for its being so deep-rooted and persistent:

a. It is relatively easy to draw attention to new achievements in the line of skill, technical efficiency, close observation, in the discovery and representation of objective truths (for instance, in perspective). On the other hand, it is difficult to make people see the more intimate, original, genuine values that are not due to our effort or industry — as, for example, the silent power of an un-divided space, its inner transparency, its radical simplicity, or the contemplative, self-forgetful spirit that absorbs the artist's whole personality and with which he is identified.

b. Naturalistic painting can display a deep fidelity to objective truth — a quality of modesty and humility, of self-abnegation, of clarity. And this is an authentic, indispensable value, the very sub-stance of art.

c. Every perception is in itself a transformation of an external stimulus into a psychic, subjective reality of thought. So, for in-stance, any perception somehow transcends the material multiplicity that we must assume to be in the stimulus. This reality of thought is all the stronger when the object is contemplatively perceived and not considered as a means to an end. Nevertheless, when this awareness of the thought itself (its rich simplicity, for instance, its spiritual transparency, its suggestion of the infinite or even of the finite as a present value) is too much dwelt upon, and the artist's heart and mind are less devoted to the things represented than to a direct search for these same qualities of thought, then an element of external construction tends to intrude on his clarity of vision. A kind of innocence is lost. On the other hand, the artist who believes he is faithfully reproducing an object — or at any rate expresses a theme that he sees as an integral part of the object — does not risk the involuntary substitution of the original qualities and modalities of the thought for these same objective qualities, shorn of their original force and falsified.

2. PRAGMATIC THEORIES. The remarkable example of Tolstoy comes at once to mind. He doubtless recognized in art the one spiritual value that could on its own strength compete with charity, could conceivably be its antagonist; hence he condemned art except insofar as it might be a vehicle for charity. In considering the relationship between art and ethics, the first point to make is this: Moral (not conventional) values are, when *active*, all of a piece with other motive-values in an encompassing kinship of values that lies at the very root of art. They are of course something quite different when they become a rule or a preconceived end for which art is supposed to serve as a means.

Pragmatism tends to see and to define *being* in its instrumentality, or as a 'function,' and not in its own true nature; and such a standard is, I think, especially inadequate in relation to art.

Pragmatic theories find the value of art in something other than artistic activity. They ask us to appreciate the usefulness of a work of art from different points of view, or they may merely point to its worldly success or failure. The artist is hardly considered in himself: what matters most is the influence of other artists on his work and the influence of his own work on present or future generations. Art is treated as a social product. Now it is obvious that no condition of time or place should be overlooked. A poet writes in his native language and this is an essential element of his art. But it is surely not his chief characteristic. He might feel much closer to a poet of another country or another age.

These theories ignore every intimate aspect of self-realization — everything that a work of art truly is in itself, everything intrinsic that can justify the worth and the name of artist. He is reduced to a link in a chain of cause and effect, to "a machine that in itself is nothing." [1] Such theories adopt the popular tendency to derive everything from something else — representing and interpreting it by some standard other than its own and, at the same time, representing it as what it is not. Artistic awareness is not plumbed to its own depths, but is rather referred to the social or the subconscious. Above all, these theories only take into account a world of objective existents, of *things* (whether material or ideal); consequently, I think they fail to penetrate the intimate nature of art and thought.

3. PHYSIOLOGICAL THEORIES. These, too, derive the value of art from something heterogeneous — that is, from something whose nature is quite different from that of art, that has no intelligible causal relation to the intrinsic value of art. They trace art back to its physical and physiological conditions. They ignore, for instance, the fact that even the sensation of sweetness we find in sugar cannot be explained by its physicochemical determinants; that sweetness contains a quality of infinitude, an inner unity, a softness and tenuity, none of which belong to a merely quantitative world.

I gather under the same heading those theories that attribute the value of art to numerical relationships. As is well known, some painters furnished the measurements of the perfect human figure. Or canons of measurement were taken from nature itself, in its lawgiving role. But it is clear that if the value of a work of art depended upon fixed measurements and proportions, anyone could produce a masterpiece. Today the effects of fixed measurements and proportions are in some way and in the final analysis attributed to certain physical and physiological laws, such as the wavelengths of colors. But ratios and numbers provide no intel-

[1] D. H. Lawrence, *Last Poems*, ed. Richard Aldington and Giuseppi Orioli (Florence: G. Orioli, 1932), p. 50.

ligible explanation of the value of art.

In the past the importance given numbers and proportions in explaining the value of art could seem less clumsy, less absurd, because the heterogeneity between quantitative and qualitative was to a degree ignored. Numbers, in fact, were endowed with a mystical or even magical quality, for instance by the Pythagoreans. And the great architects of the Renaissance (I think especially of Leon Battista Alberti and Palladio) thought that the proportions of a temple should correspond to the proportions of the human figure, because man is made in the image of God.

Nevertheless the canons of geometry did contribute indirectly to the beauty of these architects' works, because these canons probably saved them from capricious or arbitrary invention and constrained them to a certain simplicity and sobriety. Moreover, we must bear in mind that mathematical relations are conceived as infinitely necessary, and when they are intensely thought they represent a quality of intrinsic necessity — an infinite identity in multiplicity, a luminous reality of thought. Thus mathematics finds a kind of poetry in numbers.

But this kind of poetry, if we may so call it, is too one-sided to express the true and proper positivity of life, its originality forever self-renewing in the fullness of its values and modalities — the integrity of thought in its creative spontaneity. There is always a gulf between the rigid necessity of mathematical relations, however intimately and freshly felt, and that kind of inevitability that merges with the very sense of creative freedom.

Piero della Francesca was certainly the greatest and most explicit apologist for mathematics in relation to painting. What Sir Kenneth Clark writes in his excellent book seems to me conclusive, that Piero della Francesca's geometrical rules were only "an apparatus by means of which . . . [his] belief in harmony had been expressed, an apparatus so elaborate and convincing that it seemed almost to be the thing itself." [2] But, he continues, this apparatus "turned out, once the breath of life had left it, to be no nearer to the essence of art than all the other theories of prosody, of counterpoint, of prismatic colour . . . ." In another passage this author says, "We see that in the end, like all the great classic artists, he justifies the Crocean theory of art, for however carefully his work is planned, it is only in the immediate act of creation that it assumes its essential quality of new life." [3]

4. THEORIES OF EXPRESSION AS ORIGINAL REALITY. It is Croce who makes a point of using the term 'expression' to indicate the essential nature of poetic and artistic thought. This word is easily misunderstood. Yet what can be put in its place? It has the virtue of underlining the importance of the sensible element whereby thought is realized and developed. Expression means realization, actualization — not necessarily the *outward* actualization (the so-called 'execution'). It signifies *form*, if by form one means not the completed form but the formative principle itself (*active*, creative). It is an original motive-value, intimately and immediately purposive. It is thought itself in its aspect of light, rather than in its extrinsically purposive, practical and ethical, aspect. It is the value and the reality of an intimate self-realization.

Obviously expression should not be taken in the sense of a 'discharge,' as many psychologists understand it, even in reference to art. Such notions are mechanistic. Nor should we use this word to denote the signs, accents, or gestures that attract attention because they express definite states of mind. Furthermore, expression is not a symbol, not a conventional sign, and it should not be opposed

[2] *Piero della Francesca* (London: Phaidon Press, 1951), p. 55.

[3] Ibid., p. 32.

to the so-called content, with which it is all of a piece. To sum up, *expression* is a coming-to-consciousness — the attaining of consciousness by means of an intimate self-realization.

But at this point theories diverge. For Croce opposes poetic or artistic thought (in a word, 'expression,' or as he later says, 'poetic expression') to logical thought. Expression so conceived, however, would become exactly what it is not: something opaque, very one-sided, blind. To be sure, Giambattista Vico, a pioneer of the doctrine, also opposes imagination ('fantasy,' or let us just say 'expression') to logical thought. But he may have done so for polemical reasons. He was struggling against the mechanistic tendencies of a philosophy that had just begun to ape the physical sciences; he wanted to rescue the imagination (*fantasia*), the indivisible unity of body and soul, the locus of full, irreducible reality. Altogether right seems to me the position of Blake, who also extols imagination as ultimate reality and as identity of body and soul. He, however, opposes it, not to reason, but to false reason (that is, to formal logic, to abstract intellect, whenever they are abused, taken beyond their proper limits).

I do not see how it can be doubted. The profound logic of thought is the very life of poetry and art. The most subtle, delicate, remote, forgotten conceptual kinships are revealed in poetry. Expression attains its reality, above all, in the moment of an infinite opening — an unlimited need for understanding, an exigency without which the power and reality of thought are altogether lacking.

Art realizes this deeper logic, if, as we must, we also take the word logic in its etymological sense, as 'logos,' the Word. In the *poetic* or creative essence — in creative spontaneity — there is a world or a center of intrinsic truth; there is, I maintain, the whole gamut of the psyche *in nucleo*. Here we find a primordial exigency of form and essentiality — and this speaks to our understanding, implying, for example, novelty, unity, individuality, form as an infinite intimate demand, a feeling for the finite and the infinite, the seed of humility and pride, the immediacy, however indistinct, of a universally originating principle. Such values and modalities, in their necessity of intrinsic truth, make up the fabric of the imagination, and their inexhaustible discovery is its primary spring.

Creative freedom, I must insist, should not in the first place be understood as freedom of choice, but rather as true — not inertial, not altogether derived — positivity that, it is fair to assume, characterizes subjective being in all living nature. This underived element, this absolute presentness, belongs preeminently to the essence of art. For the soul of expression is a subtle motive that operates in the absolute present, not antecedently. Our awareness of it holds the sense of something eternally young, of contemplation, disinterestedness, of something like the key to all human comprehension. This is the world of art, a world of living potentialities, wherein the highest value also signifies a more radical ontological reality.

Hence a discovery of what is most profoundly native to psychic activity cannot be separated from the artist's activity. This is precisely why successive, more-or-less fortunate artistic attempts are full of interest for the history of thought and human consciousness. Consider the Impressionists: their discovery, or their new and more profound conviction, that a true impression is in itself such a remarkable reality, such a powerful revelation, is of concern not only to art but also, and very immediately, to philosophy. Because the progressive disclosure of subjectivity has always, I believe, been the true realm of philosophy.

In a cosmos in which number and quantity seem overwhelmingly predominant, art reveals quality as *ultimately real in the very actuality of consciousness.*

It really is not art alone that bears witness to value as an ultimate and primal reality, but in art this experience has a character that is distinctly cognitive (contemplative–cognitive).

We must now dwell for a moment on this subject of the contemplative–cognitive character of art. What kind of knowledge is it? It is not descriptive knowledge, but a knowledge that is *being*. And it is not knowledge of what is represented as an object, but implicit knowledge of the creative or *poetic* essence. I should like to illustrate this last point.

If we look at a beautiful painting, we have a very real sense of undivided space, intuitively perceived. It is not space as a measured background, but space that is an integral part of all things and shapes, constitutive of them. Here is a rich unity, a rich simplicity; but there is no given point at which we can grasp it analytically. This is the wonder of 'the one in the many' or 'the many in the one' — an absolute presence.

The unity of a painting is generally attributed to the unity of the so-called subject matter; it is certainly due to many different elements. I will mention the following: the organic unity of the living figures, the unmistakable significance of certain gestures, the relation of various means toward one end, a purely mechanical interplay of external conditions, contiguity, the fact that all the parts of the painting are by the same hand, uniformity, tones and overtones, identity of the material used by the artist. There is, besides, the unity that comes from the external will, the intention of the artist — a constructive rather than a creative element that we have in mind when we talk of 'composition.' But the innate creative unity is a different one. It is a rich, compact unity, an inner transparency. It transpires both in the single touch and in the vision as a whole. It conveys, as I see it, a rich positivity, an active principle of potentiality that by itself implies an inner multiplicity.

For there cannot be any real unity among determinate existents. There can be an intimate, spiritual unity only through a living potentiality that contains the sense of the possible and, therefore, of multiplicity, originally and without the need to presuppose a separate principle of synthesis.

This living potentiality, if we rightly consider it, implies a value that cannot be localized and that refuses to be measured (for anything that can even virtually be measured either *is* or *is not*; no originality, or creativity, or true positivity can find a place there). Further, this potentiality implies an underived element, an intrinsic characterization. Now what is *underived* and *intrinsically characterized* calls to mind values of an intimate and eternal nature. There are no limits to this kinship of values once we admit that something really active and not derived from elsewhere exists in the subjectivity of being. And the artist, sometimes without being wholly aware of it, is moved by such values and knows them, though this knowledge is implicit rather than explicit and objectified. I maintain that art is knowledge in this sense — that is, at one and the same time it is expression and immediate revelation of the spirit. According to an exterior point of view, the sensible form is a symbol or a sign; but it is the task of aesthetics, I think, to explain how the sensible form is both a substance and an immediate revelation of an eternal world of values.[4]

These motive-values, as I have often remarked, cannot properly be *sought*, since they must work of their own accord and find

---

[4] I have dealt with this concept in various writings, especially in *Il concetto dell'indeterminazione*, part 2, chap. 5, "L'arte come scoperta della causa attuale"; *English Poetry and Its Contribution to the Knowledge of a Creative Principle*, chap. 18, "Some Conclusions Concerning Aesthetics"; *A Philosophy of Potentiality*, part 2, "Philosophy and Art Criticism" [publication information for books by Leone Vivante cited in the text will be found at the beginning of this volume].

thereby their own kinships. Their originality is an essential principle for which there is no substitute. Hence we may understand, in part, how the artists (as it very often happens) seek minor goals even as they practice and exert and discover their power. They are, in fact, almost forced to strive for goals that do not really make up the value of their art, and they must have an absolute confidence in them; such goals are the knowledge of objective truths, new subject matter, technical devices, new materials to be used, all sorts of inventions. And this is also partly the reason why critics and art historians, no less than artists, often give such inadequate reasons for the real value of a work of art, for often all they do is inquire whether these minor goals have been attained or felicitously pursued.

I shall mention finally the hedonistic theories and views. To reduce the appreciation of a work of art to a common standard of pleasure would be a form a agnosticism. But I do not think that any consistently agnostic position exists in relation to art. One or another of the theories I have mentioned is always implied. If the pleasure is ultimately attributed to physiological causes, we fall back upon the physiological theories of art. If we base our judgment on an average or poll of opinions as to which works of art afford more or less pleasure, we fall back upon the pragmatic theories, and so it is if we take as a term of reference the market price of works of art at any given period. On the other hand, if we turn our attention to the nature of pleasure — and not to pleasure as an epiphenomenon, entirely deprived of ontological value in its subjective reality — it will be difficult not to revert to the theories of expression, which are concerned with the nature of creative spontaneity.

We must distinguish pleasure as an active subject from pleasure as an object we seek. Pleasure as an active principle may even be identified with the creative essence and with its spiritual integrity. In this sense, blessed then be the artist who follows pleasure — that is, beauty — without any preconceived theory or ambitious program. He will perhaps reach the highest pinnacle. The word 'pleasure' is often used in the sense of an active subject — as subject of the phrase in point both of logic and of grammar — and it so recurs in Dante, as in the verse "Sì che il sommo piacer gli si dispieghi," where 'pleasure' is synonymous with God.[5] On the other hand, pleasure may be conceived as an object of the will — as a thing, as a predetermined end, and not as a living quality; it is then the separate ego that comes to the foreground, and what we are faced with is a selfish attitude, a one-sided mode of being.

Today the word 'pleasure' is generally used in its objective abstract sense — as when we read about the 'amount of pleasure' we may absorb in watching a play, or about 'aesthetic pleasure.' Clumsy expressions. As far as I can see, the term 'pleasure,' in its general usage, is inadequate to signify the relatively impersonal value of creative spontaneity in art.

Let the following point illustrate what I am saying. In a work of art there is usually an *extrinsic* element that seems almost, though not absolutely, indispensable: it is the so-called 'subject' (or, as I say, 'object'); in architecture, or in ceramics, it is the 'function.' But every extrinsic element must be forgotten — surpassed and transformed by a deeper reality. Now, how could pleasure alone make us forget, for instance, the horror and atrocity of the Crucifixion and the Slaughter of the Innocents, which we often see in paintings?

---

[5] "That the Chief Pleasure be to him displayed . . ." *Paradiso*, 33. 33 [Longfellow's translation].

We say about love that it is a pleasure that is pain, a pain that is pleasure — something beyond pleasure and pain. We might say the same about artistic creation. We must recognize, however, that in art and in poetry, joy — creative joy — is, in a distinctly characteristic way, primary and immediate.

CHAPTER 2

The Ontological New and the Positivity of Being

I. ON THE USE OF CERTAIN TERMS

POTENTIALITY. According to philosophical tradition, the term potentiality' is opposed to 'actuality' and refers to the conditions necessary for what does not yet exist. But the same term is sometimes used also to mean that something is in its becoming, its making; that is, it is used in the sense of active potentiality, in a way indeterminate and yet very real.

Bradley wrote on the use of this and analogous terms, "The words 'potential,' and 'latent,' and 'nascent,' and we may add 'virtual' and 'tendency,' are employed too often. They are used in order to imply that a certain thing exists; and this, although either we ought to know, or know, that the thing certainly does not exist." [1] He severely condemns the abuse of these terms. But his conviction is perhaps not wholly unrelated to the fact that he considers the determinate the touchstone of reality.

Nicola Abbagnano understands potentiality as a mere condi-

---

[1] F. H. Bradley, *Appearance and Reality: A Metaphysical Essay* (London: S. Sonnenschein & Co.; New York: Macmillan Co., 1908), p. 384.

tion. And, in contrast, he uses the term 'possible' not in opposition to what is real and actual but as signifying the real life of actuality. I too have used the word 'possible' in this sense, for instance, even so early as in my *Principles of Ethics*: "What offends us in our not yet actualized being, in our 'possibility,' offends us more than what offends us in our present and formed existence; what contrasts with and destroys our hopes, more than what damages us today: and this is because our true reality is not only the act, in its exclusiveness, but an infinite of the possible, infinitely present and creative." [2] And it has always seemed extraordinary and almost incredible to me that this meaning of the 'possible' should be ignored or neglected by philosophers. And so it has been very encouraging for me to have found in Abbagnano, a philosopher and historian of philosophy, such authoritative confirmation. It is Abbagnano who writes, "The category of the possible is the most used and at the same time the most disregarded by philosophers." [3] If I am not presuming too much, Abbagnano and I have reached, independently, similar convictions.

However, I prefer the term 'potentiality' (or 'virtuality') to designate being as active power-to-be, as *exigency* or urge to be, rather than 'possibility' or 'the possible,' or other terms, for the following reasons:

1. In everyday speech the possible is usually sharply opposed to whatever has reality. The intimate force of the Latin *posse* is lost. 'Potentiality,' on the other hand, still lends itself to expressing the idea of having power (the notion conveyed by the English verb *to be able*) in its indeterminate and actual value. One can talk about 'living potentiality' — not nearly so well can one talk about

[2] Pages 35–36.

[3] Nicola Abbagnano, *Possibilità e libertà* (Turin: Taylor, 1956), p. 212.

'living possibility'—and (in philosophical usage) of 'active potentiality,' where the expression 'active possibility' would not give the immediate sense and would need interpretation.

2. The term 'possible' can have, I shall say, a neutral meaning: that is, it can refer to an abstract alternative, to a condition of indifference between the power to be and not to be, between the power to create and not to create. Or it may be concerned with mere objective reality, as if, for example, I said, "It may be (it's possible) that our friend missed the train." The term 'potentiality,' on the other hand, expresses or lends itself to expressing *being* as an *exigency*, as an immanent finality or purposiveness in the sense of being, even as an obstinacy of being. The possible is neutral in regard to being and not being: potentiality brings to mind the idea of being as immediately final in itself — against the prevailing mechanistic trend.

3. When one says, for example, that a plant is 'potentially' or 'in potency' in the seed, one might simply be stating that in the seed there are the conditions necessary and sufficient for the formation of the plant (except for the secondary or other conditions that one can surely count upon and on which one need not fix one's attention). It is, then, certainly an inaccurate way of speaking, especially since one is convinced that in point of fact the plant is not in the seed. But one may also mean something else. I don't here intend to talk about typical form-processes, of prototypes or of metaorganisms. But there are intrinsic values and modalities of psychic reality that may be found, in a more or less specific way, either in the seed or in the plant. They will not be literally the same ones, but *essentially* they will be the same. Now the above-mentioned expressions may contain an implicit, even though unconscious, reference to this powerful originality–intrinsicality of

characters, to a reality of principle or of essence — which is fundamentally the reality, as well as the problem, of the psyche.

4. The term 'potentiality' (active potentiality) expresses and
makes intimately intelligible the unity–multiplicity that characterizes any moment of psychic reality. For, to my way of thinking,
it is a mistake to postulate a distinct principle supposedly necessary
to make oneness out of the many. Essentially multiplicity does not
preexist. Thus, for example, in an effort, each moment is immediately a tendency or psychic tension (hence multiplicity, psychic
extension) and also an undivided reality. Now this *undivided*
quality of psychic reality, which reduces to oneness the perceived
material multiplicity, becomes convincing for us, and we almost
touch it with our hand as a reality that we have experienced —
ultimate and actual — precisely in the sentiment of a living potentiality. Potentiality is unity in an infinite opening. Naturally this
unity–multiplicity is revealed also in 'freedom,' in 'power,' in hope,
in love, in hate . . . and truly the same *undivided* is implicit in all
the terms of the psyche. But the other terms don't reveal to the
same extent its radical, original reality.

Potentiality, far from being a superfluous or insidious term, is
the origin of our sense of the infinite.

INFINITE. There is objective infinity, there is mathematical
infinity, and there is the infinite as absolute universality — to
which the 'finite' things of this world are contrasted. But everyday (and poetic) language has yet another use for this term
'infinite.' We say, for example, infinite sorrow, infinite torment,
infinite patience, infinite joy or hope, infinite rest or resonance,
infinite love or desire or remorse, infinite sadness, infinite affection.
This inner infinite is a fundamental reality — and is not at all

subordinate to objective infinity, which is almost its shadow or its metaphor.

The concept of the objective infinite requires only that the exigency of going beyond the limits be conceived as logically stronger than that of setting a limit, or of representing to us a limit, and we can well conceive an endless numeration of given data. But the inner or inward infinite wants nothing less than our giving up the idea that the determinate existent makes up and exhausts in itself the real.

The inner or subjective infinite seeks a point of reference or foothold in objective infinity, whether spatial or temporal, whether in the infinitely great or the infinitely small, and its value is in part due to this objective infinity. But it is above all the inner infinite, active in itself, that gives value to objective infinity. Outside of this inner or dynamic, never-accomplished infinite there is nothing but dead and abstract objectivity. The inner infinite doesn't involve primarily the idea that something in fact exists beyond every limit, but rather the immediate exigency of this transcending of the limit. "He loves not at all who loves *enough*." Or again, "I will always love you and it will never be possible to love you more": for even the infinite in the act declines everything that is measure, limit, division, number. It is transcendence — insatiable, without end — of its own form. And its immediate, intimate value is that of active potentiality that is *being* itself. Its spring is not in objective infinity.

Nor can one, except in a spirit of blind transcendence, reserve the word 'infinite' to mean the Absolute and therefore describe as 'finite' every earthly thing. The infinite is a phenomenal reality. It is a reality of experience if it is anything. Reputation, honor, shame draw their strength from the inner infinite. Words, paintbrush, chisel express the given as an infinite of itself, in an endlessly open transparency. Without this inner infinite there would be neither fear, nor terror, nor hope, nor life. Whoever kills the tiniest creature shatters an *infinite* — an inner or intrinsic infinite, a reality which not anything that is determinate can give.

Life clings to the determinate, the objectively existent, static, inert, divisible, measurable reality. But this is not its reality. The reality of life is in something intense and intent, in an infinite demand or exigency, that comes alight in every element of inertia. It is in an almost awesome intrinsicality of character that challenges objective time and space, exists only in its perennial originality, and certainly cannot be identified with objective infinity.

'Infinite silence' is not primarily an objective infinite: it expresses the soul as a demand exceeding any form, as much as it is possible — a radical *potentiality*.

And therefore, and notwithstanding an authoritative opinion to the contrary, it seems to me that we should not describe the immediate feeling of the possible as 'finite'; and I do not hesitate to use the word 'infinite' according to what is perhaps its most common usage in everyday language, in the sense of the subjective infinite — in other words, 'active,' 'creative,' 'effective,' 'intimate,' 'intensive,' 'qualitative,' 'dynamic,' 'of tendency' . . .

DETERMINATE. Here, too, I shall quote Bradley, who says, almost by way of an axiom, "It is certain that, with increase in determinateness, a thing becomes more and more real." [1] And in fact we do think generally of reality as ultimately determinate, and only apparently and provisionally indeterminate. But isn't an anxious wait reality? And yet it is indeterminate. Will a portrait by Rembrandt have less reality than a painting that goes into the minutest detail? And won't fear be so much the stronger the more

[1] *Appearance and Reality*, p. 494.

indeterminate it is, not only in regard to itself but also the object? Even with reference to matter, this proposition, "the more determinate, the more real," does not seem valid. Is an elementary particle less determinate than a molecule? It would be difficult to answer; but, in any case, the particle would not be less real because of this. One supposes matter to have always the same degree of reality.

But I shall quote a more recent author, Jacques Jalabert, who equally, and according to generally accepted opinion, considers that the *determinate* represents the ultimate criterion of reality. He writes, "Réalité et indétermination sont des termes qui s'excluent. On ne peut pas être, sans être en même temps ceci ou cela, ceci à l'exclusion de cela." [5] Brittle words, because they don't take into account the fact that the determinate is one thing, the unique and the distinct and the individual another, and because they treat the nature of being as settled: for if (subjective) being is not objectively determinate, the fact of being "this to the exclusion of that" does not change its nature.

For example, *this* assertion of mine has reality and value in the presence of indefinite possibilities that it excludes, and yet these are inseparable from the assertion itself, and not by virtue of a formal implication, but immediately, and they are all one with its strength. My reason is all in play, my reason infinitely, in consequence of an intimate demand for comprehension over and beyond any given limit. The 'this,' in its material existentiality, or abstract ideality, is certainly something analytically reachable, divisible, measurable, exactly comparable, strictly determinate:

[5] "Reality and indetermination are mutually exclusive terms. One cannot be without being at the same time this or that, this to the exclusion of that." *L'un et le multiple; de la critique à l'ontologie* (Paris: Presses Universitaires de France, 1955), p. 76.

but, as a reality of thought, it is an infinite 'not that,' a boundless arc of identity.

Determinate, finite reality belongs to form's materiality and to our abstract scheme of reality. But without a doubt the term has varied significance.

With reference to matter and to the abstract objective scheme, 'determinate' signifies the same concept that, in various respects, may be expressed in other words as 'finite,' 'precise,' 'measurable,' 'superimposable,' and so on. In reference to will it may mean, for example, 'decided,' 'sure,' 'definite,' 'unequivocal,' or 'resolute.' In French and English, words of that derivation are often used in this sense: for instance, 'une volonté la plus déterminée,' or in English 'determination' in the sense of firm decision, of resolute character, and so forth. In Italian this acceptation of the term is rare. In reference to form it may mean 'distinct,' 'sculptured,' 'perspicuous,' 'cutting,' 'incisive,' 'concrete,' 'finite.' But here the 'finite' (as well as the other terms) is not intended in an abstractly objective sense, but rather it expresses a value of form that is identically *infinite exigency* of form.

Here I intend using this word 'determinate' in the sense of materially determinate or of objectively determinate according to the objective abstract scheme. It seems to me that, especially in considering the problem of indeterminacy, one should use the word 'determinate' in the specific sense it has when it describes an objectively rigorous reality of relation. Moreover, any other acceptation of the word has a varied and uncertain significance.

NECESSITY AND FREEDOM. It seems incredible how often well-known philosophers use the term 'necessity' without making it clear whether they mean necessity in the broad sense, generic, ontologically uncompromising, or whether they mean mechanical, or formal, or geometric, or mathematical necessity; or whether, quite in opposition, they mean the intrinsic necessity that identifies itself with freedom. In consideration of the crucial problem of whether in the world there is nothing but mechanism, force of inertia, and total derivation, or whether, on the contrary, there is also a principle of true, real productivity, creativity, something originally active, obviously the term 'necessity' must be treasured.

Mechanical necessity is necessity *par excellence*, necessity, I shall say, in the strict sense of the word. In each one of its moments it is relative to something else: but, in its relativity, it is absolute, rigid, literal. It is intended as that which is entirely abstracted from the thought that thinks it.

Mathematical truths have the character of strict, literal necessity as long as one considers their objective reality, and as long as one is removed from the thought behind them: but as reality of thought any truth is always an infinite of itself, an actual value of infinite possibility and capability of verification, an exigency of universality, whose measure is not given. And this non-predetermination — whether real, or whether, if you will, only apparent — is all one with its strength. In this way, a mathematical truth, as a reality of thought, will, right from the start, always differ according to the larger or smaller awareness of the value of universality of a given formula. Even a mathematical truth will always be thought with greater or lesser conviction, faith, novelty, contemplation, or as a mere instrument, and so forth. And the measure of this conviction is rigorously predetermined, that is *sub judice*. The very force of this conviction seems to indicate an intrinsically final, purposive value that would be superfluous and absurd in automatism.

Necessity in the strict sense — which is also its ordinary and obvious meaning — is well represented in its characteristic aspect by Abbagnano, where he says, "Necessity does not contain the indication of any value: it is there because it is." [6]

I call 'intrinsic necessity' that which implies intrinsic finality or purposiveness. The biologist frowns at the mere mention of purposiveness, and immediately thinks of angels and devils. He means by purposiveness only extrinsic purposiveness. But the fundamental principle of purposiveness is intrinsic purposiveness, from which the extrinsic can, intelligibly, derive. In extrinsic purposiveness (as limit–concept) the end is a given object; in intrinsic purposiveness (equally as limit–concept) the end is an active motive value, which is identified with the agent–subject. Intrinsic purposiveness is the very *being*, conceived as exigency, as affirmation, or as negation (which is still affirmation), or also as unyielding pertinacity of being, which, in specific forms, may actuate itself in effects perhaps no less rigorously foreseeable than those of mechanical necessity, but which is of an altogether different nature.

I shan't here go into the various meanings of the term 'freedom.' In its more radical aspect, the concept of freedom, I believe, may be identified with that of a true and real positivity of subjective being. Freedom is intrinsic to (subjective) being, or it never *is*. Swinburne says: "Free — and we know not another as infinite word." [7] Naturally the term 'infinite' here designates a dynamic infinite or an infinite of tendency: no one can think of an objectively absolute freedom — a concept in itself contradictory like that of omnipotence. Freedom not only needs a network of conditions to nourish it, qualify it, and activate it, but above all it arises bearing the weight, so to speak, the intimate tie, of its own intrinsic

[6] *Possibilità e libertà,* p. 105.

[7] Algernon Charles Swinburne, "A Child's Future"; cf. my *English Poetry and Its Contribution to the Knowledge of a Creative Principle,* p. 298.

nature, which is infinity, individuality, responsibility, potentiality, essential newness.

II.　CONCERNING CERTAIN OBJECTIONS TO THE CONCEPT OF BECOMING AS ULTIMATE REALITY

Ex NIHILO NIHIL FIT. Exterior facts, in my judgment, do not demonstrate decisively either determinism or indeterminism. Even the great phenomenon of reproductivity in living nature, through which typical processes are repeated in very similar forms, under different conditions, either contemporaneously or successively, though it rests on rigid physicochemical causal relationships, leaves room for the hypothesis of a kind of obstinacy, of a mental nature, regarding which the problem of indeterminacy remains open. To my way of thinking, the strongest arguments against indeterminacy are, as I have said before, of a logical nature.[8]

"Every change must have its sufficient reason, its cause," *ex nihilo nihil fit*. Abstract reason — here I mean primarily materialism, mechanism — explains change in the easiest way, that is, by denying it as an ultimate reality by reducing it to preexistent elements, formally identical with themselves, and by admitting only spatial or spatio-temporal shifts — these, too, all derived.[9]

Let us consider a moment of effort — if, for example, I exercise with the dynamometer. If I touch the hundred-and-one mark rather than one hundred, the difference is largely due to given conditions, to chance (that is, to innumerable and incalculable causes or to causes only indirectly connected with my effort), to the

---

[8] See my *Philosophy of Potentiality*, chap. 1.

[9] Cf. Emile Meyerson, *De l'explication dans les sciences*, 2 vols. (Paris: Payot, 1921), in several places, particularly 1:127.

condition of my health, to the level of my fatigue, and so forth. But there is something essential in my effort that refuses to feel entirely necessitated, or, on the other hand, fortuitous, because it is felt as merit, value, faith, power, and constancy. It is felt as a positivity implying essentially a negative possibility. Its intensity seems, right to the last, *not* given, and this *appearance* is a vital and absolutely essential factor of my effort. We feel that in a specified center or circuit there are infinite points at which it could culminate, and the culmination at this or that point does not depend on, or does not only depend on, chance, or on necessity, but rather on an undivided reality of tension whose essence is to overwhelm endlessly any imagined limit.

The exact point of maximum efficiency of my effort at a given moment, as indicated by the dynamometer's needle, concerns the result, the measurable efficacy, but it does not affect the intimate nature of the effort. Any measurement, whether predetermined, or even existing only in the present moment, would stifle, would exclude effort; it would reduce it to a group of determinate objective existents, in which any creativity, any real becoming, is excluded. For everything that *exists* either exists or it does not exist: there is no place for real, true positivity, that is, for such *being* as can be conceived as exigency, as activity originally active. In fact, effort cannot be reduced to existents. Any measurement that represented effort entirely would turn it into something objectively given, analytically apprehensible, divisible, a group of externally conditioned elements, incapable of intimate unity and creativity.

One may reply that if measurement does resolve effort into a group of determinate objective existents, incapable of ultimate becoming and of *originality*, nothing is demonstrated since one denies that this originality exists. Also, one may reply that, certainly, if one knew the exact result of effort, then that very effort would be superfluous: it would lack any incentive; but the fact is that we do not have the knowledge or exact foresight of the causes and the result, and this suffices! One may equally reply that, even admitting that there is an original causality, no explanation is offered why this — even apart from all the cause-conditions of actuation — should or could have in itself the sufficient reason of diversity. And further, one may reply that the *posse*, the capacity for effort, effort itself, must have some measure; that there must be an inner limit, and therefore a measure. Here we may counter, however, by saying that the idea of omnipotence seems to indicate that a measureless reality is not unthinkable. As is apparent, we are at sea.

Chance as an absolutely fortuitous event does not concern us. Indeterminacy is generally taken by physicists as (absolute) chance, or as a mixture of (absolute) chance and literal necessity. But, to begin with, chance is neither value nor freedom — not any more so than strict necessity; and it has nothing to do with the active indeterminacy of which I am speaking. And further, (absolute) chance is an extremely difficult concept. Any absolute beginning must seemingly be the beginning of an immensity of things inextricably knitted together — whether matter or psychic reality is concerned. When physical reality is concerned, the relation: chance = creation, comes as less shocking because the scientist generally uses the word 'creation' very casually and in a very broad, uncritical sense, without considering the implications of the term, and without any claim as to its intelligibility; and because in physical reality it is perhaps possible to conjecture an element that is not radically a part of the nature of the whole. But in psychic reality the element of noninertia is, even in embryo, I maintain, the central and supreme moment and an inexhaustible implication of values, an indivisible node of values and modalities.

Any psychic moment contains a negative possibility — in the very act of excluding that possibility; without it, it would fall into literal necessity and mechanism. Nicola Abbagnano uses various words to designate this negative possibility: 'indeterminacy,' 'instability,' 'uncertainty,' 'precariousness,' 'caducity,' 'danger,' 'risk';[10] 'dubious,' 'problematic' (p. 210); 'ambiguous,' 'undecided' (p. 211); and he contrasts this uncertainty with what he aptly calls 'ontological stiffening' (p. 59). One could add other terms, for instance, suspense, awaiting, threat, hope. But all these terms, although it is difficult to substitute others for them, remain ever inadequate to define a *negative* that is inseparable from the *positive*, and that is wholly one with its strength. And perhaps it might actually be preferable to use the positive term, since *certainty* itself would have no intimate meaning without a 'negative' that it contains at the very point at which it excludes or dominates it. Without the 'negative,' certainty would have no dimension or psychic reality, but would be only the certainty of a mechanical instrument.

Any decision that is not automatic contains this negative possibility. The most resolute affirmation is an infinite — not formal — identity with its own self against difficulties and objections, actual or eventual, definite or indefinite, and inexhaustible, that converge to form its content.[11]

Freedom is not in the abstract choice, in the abstract alternative, but in the prevailing of a motive, with which we identify. Even in the sphere of indifference, what moves us is a motive-

----

[10] *Possibilità e libertà*, p. 58.

[11] Cf. *supra*, under "Determinate." As Abbagnano says further: "Any definition of a term or of a principle makes no sense except in view of the possibility that that term or that principle be intended with a meaning different from the defined one." *Possibilità e libertà*, p. 212.

value that, like any motive-value, is a motive or moment of intrinsic finality, intrinsic purposiveness; whether it be impatience, desperation, pride, rebellion, or caprice. A fundamental motive of which we are often hardly aware is the feeling of responsibility — sense or feeling of responsibility, whose measure is not given. Freedom generally presents itself in the form of a not-being-able-to-be-but-*that*, as opposed to a being-able-to-be-something-else, which it negates, and which it nevertheless in some way contains.

Freedom implies the new, the ontological new, which is a real and true becoming.[12] It needs to be stressed that no vortex or whirlwind, no speed, no subtle invisible energy is inapprehensible — incapable of measure, division, objective determinate existentiality — in the sense in which the ontological new is inapprehensible. The fundamental difference, in respect to the problem of becoming, is not between, on the one hand, immobility, and, on the other, movement, but between immobility and movement on the one hand and, on the other, becoming as ultimate reality. Even if we maintain, with Heraclitus, that everything flows, that there is nothing unchangeable, not even in elementary particles, we are still a long way from ontological becoming: from creativity, from a real and true positivity, from *noninertia*. For 'originality,' 'creativity,' 'freedom,' and, finally, all the words of the spirit not to be empty words, we must face the difficult concept of a negative absolutely inherent in positivity; we must conceive of something other than objectively determinate reality.

THE CONSTANCY OF BEING. Historically, however, the principle argument against the idea of a becoming conceived as an absolute stems from our setting up as an unchanging, and therefore extra-temporal, entity the constant intrinsic character of being and value.

---

[12] I mean always 'ontological' *a parte subjecti.*

This unchanging principle would be the basis of any original value, which then, in its transitory aspect, would not reveal to us its true nature.

Value is always essentially activity, for psychic reality is ever a transforming of the crude multiplicity of the stimulus into the undivided of a power, however rudimentary. But more especially, because its reality is in the immediate light of discovery, in the infinite opening whenever it forms itself, before it is extinguished in the formed, inert form. The potentiality–positivity of value is in itself time: intimate time, time that is essentially, not only factually, irreversible; and nothing is more false than pretending to explain value according to an extratemporal reality that has nothing to do with it.

The positivity of which we are speaking may be represented as an 'eternal origin': and this expression is not in itself contradictory, because the first term is subordinate to the second and is dependent upon it. The perennial originality of the spirit cannot be canceled by any apparent immutability. The *intrinsic* or *eternal* cannot be 'entified' into an extratemporal reality. The *new* bears with it *ab aeterno* an overpowering intrinsicality, which does not annul it since it is born from it.

Often we mean that something is unchangeable only in a sort of center or root: who speaks of an unchangeable love will mean that it is always new and varied, though unchangeable in what is most radical, most fundamental, in that same love. *But that which, in order to be, needs to renew itself is the very ultimate essence!* Love is an almost awesome *simplicity* in which the particular subject is lost, and this simplicity is essentially and typically peculiar to the creative moment: a purification, an absolute redemption in the new.

There can be a continuous uniform *new*, a new without perceptible change. So it is in ecstasy. We must indeed inferentially admit that ecstasy is not stasis. The intimate unity or absolute presence of a moment of ecstasy implies potentiality *in actu*. Moreover if a nuance of variation arises in ecstasy, will the nature of ecstasy suddenly change? Will time suddenly arise? It is not likely: ecstasy will, before as after, be a perpetual new, absolute positivity, active quality.

As I have repeatedly maintained, the constancy of principles stems from the very originality of being in its supremely intrinsic characterization. If to justify this constancy we resort to the hypothesis of our identification with an active potentiality of vaster scope, cosmic, the problem is shifted, but its solution will not differ. If the problem is directed to God, as it has been said that God exists only by creating, so it may be said that its intrinsic nature does not exist outside the creative act. The problem, the mystery, the miracle, is the *supremely intrinsic* characterization of subjectivity. It is an eternity gathered into itself — "self-enshrined eternity," says Shelley, who, unless I am mistaken, describes in these terms exactly that positivity of being in its tremendous intrinsicality of character, conceived as absolutely immanent.[13]

The *nonstatic* immutability (or immobility!), asserted with reference especially to theological problems, is not intelligible other than as a constancy that is perpetually born from the potent intrinsic characterization of the ontological new — that is, of being as an ever originally active and, ultimately, intransmissible quality: any other immutability is static, has the obvious meaning of these terms 'immutable' and 'immobile'; and, more generally, outside the theological field, it excludes the new and the individual in the name of a false universality.

[13] "The Daemon of the World," v. 439.

REFERENCE TO OTHER DIFFICULTIES. As one may often read, the necessity of counterbalancing entropy offers a favorable argument for the idea of a subjective, biological principle of creation; and, on the other hand, the leveling of energy, through infinite time, presents an acute problem that cannot be put aside. But for the argument to be a valid one, subjectivity would have to be almost coexistent with the physical universe: I won't say derived from matter, but latent in it, wholly or partially constitutive of it. And before venturing into these hypotheses, one must beware skipping too casually over the apparent abyss between psychic and physical reality.

There is yet another difficulty, or at least another objection, that the concept of the ontological new runs up against: it implies creation of force, therefore an infraction of the law of conservation of energy.[14]

III. BEING AS POTENTIALITY IN ACT

BEING AS EXIGENCY OF BEING. Being bears not-being in its heart, in its most alive, most pure actuality.[15] It is this that makes its positivity and its psychic dimension. Even the expression 'come to be' is, strictly, deceiving: not-being (and therefore the *ex nihilo*, the new, positivity) does not essentially refer to a preceding moment, but belongs entirely to the actual nature of being. Nor, on the other hand, could one conceive potentiality as something midway between not-being and being, as a lesser being, a *minus ens*, that produces being. One would fall back into extrinsic causality, into a process that ultimately excludes coming into being.

[14] See "Potentiality and Objectivity" in this chapter, *infra.*
[15] I always mean the *subjective, active* being.

The objectively determinate existent — element or condition in the chain of causes and effects — I repeat, exists, or does not exist, and does not know *being*. But being that is active in itself, that in itself has substance, that is self-sustaining, is immediate exigency of being, or, more simply, *exigency*. This term 'exigency,' as here intended, means: (1) dynamically indeterminate reality; (2) intrinsic finality or purposiveness; (3) undivided reality; (4) subjectivity (that is, actual, not inert, activity).

The practical spirit calls reality the actuation that is accomplished, objectively determinate, made through exterior relations; but true being lies in the indeterminate and dynamic infinite of an exigency without which the same actuation or form would have neither unity nor reality, other than that of material multiplicity.

I must recognize that this relation: 'being=exigency of being,' is not, generally, suggested, and is even less demonstrated, by our direct intimate experience. For the most part we feel being as something we passively submit to. It is nonetheless true that being is felt as exigency in the face of danger or in agony. And what is this strange instinct for preservation of ours if not being as exigency? The so-called instinct for preservation is not properly an 'instinct.' Thus, if by instinct we mean a process largely guided by specific physiological reactions, the maternal instinct is an instinct when the mother bares her breast to the child; but motherly love is not, as the language confirms, precisely an instinct. Sexual love is an instinct, inasmuch as it depends largely, for instance, on age and sex; but the passion of love, as the language confirms, is not properly an instinct. Similarly the instinct for preservation, in my view, is not always well represented as an instinct, for it is life itself, in an intelligible aspect, the incoercible positivity of being. The exigency of being, of maintaining oneself in being — if it isn't an impulse proceeding by force of inertia — perpetually implies a negative possibility, the not-being, and the essential new. In the terror of creatures, a tremendous *positivity* of life is manifested. And in artistic creation, what is form, if it isn't exigency of form?

But this concept, in its absoluteness, has a basis of character that I shall call inferential; that is, it depends principally on: (1) its interpretive value at the root of ethical, logical, aesthetic, and biological reality; and (2) that which leaves no alternative other than a world of total derivation and inertia.

THE IMMEDIACY OF THE ONE. The intimate unity of any psychic moment may be represented by various names and expressions: the one in many, the many in one, absolute presence, *unitas multiplex*, inner transparency, simplicity in the multiple . . . . [16] No extremely rapid movement between one point and another could explain to us this absolute ubiquity. And, to say something less obvious but not less certain, between existents in their objective, finite determinacy there can be exterior relations: never, intelligibly, real unity. We are therefore confronted with a most singular principle, to the surprise and scandal of our analytical minds, which do not admit the *simple* — perhaps because the simple is not something that we can construct and reconstruct at will.

We couldn't rest at peace in the presence of this phenomenon — this absolute presence or copresence in a sensation as much as in a vision or in reasoning — unless we were to ignore it or unless it were entirely to escape our notice, except for the fact that it is intelligible to us *in that which we know most* — in what is called 'power to,' 'freedom,' 'potentiality' (active), or also 're-

---

[16] *'Présence absolue,' 'unitas multiplex'*: cf. Raymond Ruyer, *Néofinalisme* (Paris: Presses Universitaires de France, 1952), p. 14; also, *La gènese des formes vivantes* (Paris: Flammarion, 1958), pp. 64, 238, passim.

sponsibility,' 'love,' 'hate' . . . Indeed, all the names of psychic reality express, imply, or render, now more, now less explicitly, something immediately ubiquitous. The *posse*, in its radical indeterminacy, is at the same time an undivided and an extended (comprehensive, psychically extended) reality. Indivisibility in physics is a poorly understood, scarcely intelligible concept—even though in reference to the atom it was accepted without difficulty for millennia — but in psychic reality, primarily in the *posse*, there is an intelligible indivisibility.

As I have often stressed in other writings, the postulation of a distinct principle of synthesis is not necessary, and false. The very term 'synthesis' is misleading. In the actuality of consciousness there are, essentially, no parts that must be unified. Thus, as I have said, a moment of effort is in every least part of its substance immediately progressive (multiple) and undivided. Thus a moment of freedom, which is active potentiality, is immediately and identically undivided reality and psychic breadth. The principle of synthesis, presupposed or superimposed, or in any way distinct, falsifies all our conceptions of psychic reality. In the first place, it presents sensation as an element of construction inert in itself; and it prevents the recognition of simplicity as a fundamental reality in the life of the spirit—and presumably also in the least sensation.

POTENTIALITY AND OBJECTIVITY. 'Potentiality': I mean always active potentiality. 'Objectivity': I mean abstract objectivity, the formal abstract scheme. This objectivity is sometimes confused with the other objectivity, which has an altogether different nature, and which is a value of universality, a supreme subjectivity.

Potentiality describes being as exigency, in its radical indeterminacy, and with a certain sense of impersonality — without however losing, but rather stressing, a value of centrality or unity. It discovers a secret of the infinite that is in *self-making*. As I have mentioned, other terms express or immediately imply the same concept, but they present some disadvantage. Thus 'creation' may suggest the idea of a creation *ab extra*, which is creation without intimate participation (identification) of the creating principle in the thing created, and, as a limit–concept, is a mere construction on given elements — exclusion of any originality. 'Original causality,' 'actual cause,' assert the concept of an essential new more than they intimately clarify it. 'Freedom' is a term often used with strict reference to man. 'Will,' in a specific sense, concerns extrinsic finality, the putting of the means to service toward a determined end, rather than creative spontaneity.

Psychic reality is always potentiality because thought always immediately translates the reality of the stimulus, whatever it is, into a reality that is a possible infinite of itself. Such is immobility itself. Immobility, when thought, is an infinite. It is infinite potentiality, not of the thing, but of the thought that thinks it. Here too the determinate and the finite belong to the object, not to the thought, not to the living reality.

The determinate — the finite — as limit–concept, is a static residue, incapable of intimate efficiency, devoid of the immediate sense of the possible, a mere condition of something else, without original value — even though it presents utilitarian, instrumental, or conventional, and, above all, fixed values.

It is understood that the term 'to exist' is also used in a more comprehensive and no less fundamental meaning than 'being' itself: but in a specific sense, and in contrast to 'being,' it indicates any point in the extrinsic causal sequence. Its characteristic, in this meaning, is determinacy. Another characteristic is its having only one degree of reality — devoid of value in itself, and absolute in its relativity.

IV. THE ROSE OF VALUES

There is an implication of values inherent in the concept of true positivity, that is, in the concept of a reality that is not merely derivative or fortuitous. Even in the most remote part of the universe, this *positivity* or original causality will contain, intelligibly, though maybe only germinally, this rich implication or kinship of values. It may be value of actuation (form); it may be undivided presence (potentiality); it may be affirmation (intrinsic finality or purposiveness); it may be principle of individuation (unicity); it may be value of intrinsic necessity in these and other characters (value of universality). Through the concept of the ontological *new*, to my way of thinking, these values disclose, or allow us to know better, their kinships and their nature.

A person's individuality does not essentially depend on a constant indistinct background of permanent qualities, or on memory. What constitutes individual identity and continuity is the ever-new exigency of assuming in the actuality of the present all past, present, and future conditions, beyond any fixed limit. But this irreplaceable *present* could not identify itself in past experiences and reanimate them, nor could it anticipate future ones, except that the positivity–potentiality that constitutes it is immediately such a germinal implication of values and such an exigency of infinite feasibility that it is a powerful principle of interpretation and identification.

Individuality is not a *state*: it is a vital infinite, it is an intensity. It is potentiality. There is in individuality always something that exceeds any collection of data. In the living knowledge of an indeterminate potentiality each one of us becomes more deeply aware of himself, feels his own infinite, and his own loneliness, and his own individuality.

If positivity–potentiality reveals a principle of true origin that breaks the absolute uniformity and rigidity of the chain of cause and effect, then it makes intelligible for us the arising of individuality. It makes more comprehensible diversity in living nature — and the differentiation of individuals and of peoples — as not due simply to external or mechanistically conceived causes. The unrepeatable unicity of an act and individuality would be very strange products in a world of existents all equally necessitated. But for positivity to be what it really is, its degree of intensity needs not to be predetermined but rather always essentially new, never literally identical — except through coincidence, and never essentially. If the *new* were an *illusory reality*, individuality too would be an illusory reality.

In originality there is a living sense of intrinsic necessity that transcends the single act. Intrinsic necessity, as here understood (and as I have explained), implies intrinsic purposiveness, exigency, affirmation; on the other hand, necessity in the ordinary sense is necessity of relation, without a reality of its own. Now we know this intrinsic necessity as a value of the infinite, as a value of universality, as a value of eternity, as an intimate principle of truth (intrinsic truth, truth of essence, truth of principle).

And I think it is still this same intrinsicality of the nature of being in its perennial originality that in the course of history and in the wave of time appears to us at times as an awesome necessity, compared to which mechanical necessity is a simple game. And so too in the idea of fate: for the idea of fate, particularly for the ancients, does not represent, as it has been asserted, an ingenuous, apt anticipation of the legality of physical laws. 'Fate' — and the same may be said for the terms 'destiny,' 'predestination,' 'fatality' — generally expresses an altogether different concept than that of determinism, even though in practical matters these concepts may be equivalent, and even though in theory they may at times be confused.

Active potentiality, in its vital indeterminacy, makes intelligible what there is of the delicate, tender, fresh, fugitive, and yet formidable, in the rough trunk of inanimate existentiality.

There is a quality of innocence and purity in the first growing and blooming, and it would be quite wrong to ignore its probable ontological import. The lively unity, the perfect integrity, the luminous opening of an eternal birth reflect originary causality in its value of form and infinity. The ineffable grace of living forms in the renewing virginity of growing, budding, and blossoming depends on an implication of values inherent to being in its originality. There is, if I am not mistaken, in this simplicity, in this spiritual integrity, in this perfection not of an automaton, there is in youth the prevailing of the eternal over the derivative.

By 'eternal' — and by 'underived,' and by 'uncaused' — I mean not what literally has always been, but what (if it has always been) has always been originally; what is perpetually origin, not consequence. Here two views oppose one another. Historicism in its extreme forms wants to derive everything. "With patience and with time everything can be done. Things can be explained if they can be reconstructed as in a mechanical game . . . ; if they can be reduced to minimal, insignificant, obvious things that need no explanation . . ." But these things do not exist. The principal reality does not derive from other facts. There is a creative spontaneity whose value, by definition, is not derivative. Now value, as an ultimate datum, certainly presents something more mysterious than mechanism or the mere fact of relation. And we must certainly not court mystery. But perhaps it is useless to hide the truth from ourselves, and in any case this isn't the task of the philosopher or the scientist. The ontological *new* — the sense of a true origin — evokes eternity. And this cannot be said of something that has been *learned*, nor of what is instinctive, nor of what is fortuitous, nor of what is constructed, nor of the mere novelty of change.

The same essential *new* explains the nature of judgment, whether it be moral, or aesthetic, or logical. Moral judgment has no value and no reality if it is a mere construction on rules: it must be, ultimately, new, unprejudiced, not *constructed*. We must certainly keep in mind all the rules, canons, principles, traditions, authorities, examples, and we will never be cautious enough in trusting an immediate inner light, but there is no other way: we must finally be ready to give up even our dearest convictions and approach the concrete case with a virgin mind in order that our judgment may be free, and *so* have reality. The same may be said for aesthetic and logical judgment. Even when bound to a chain of formal logic, we cannot truly reach a conclusion unless we are able to give to the whole body of deductions a look free from all suspensions and bonds. Except in practical matters, no automation may serve as a substitute for this rebellion against the inert, a rebellion that is of the essence of reason. "But this *new*, this 'rebellion,' " it may be said, "will it not be arbitrary and violent?" Now then, I am eager to observe, what I say is based on the fact that the essential new is not a *tabula rasa*, even apart, it is clear, from acquired notions, from customs, education, and other admitted factors. Reason, at that very same point in which it is rebellion against what is *imposed*,[17] is need or exigency of identification ad infinitum with the real, through thought's modalities and intrinsic values, and, if it is possible, beyond these. In such a need, through which it transcends the particular subject, reason partici-

---

[17] Cf. Abbagnano, *Possibilità e libertà*, pp. 83–86.

pates in the nature of love, and in every high sense of responsibility.

In this *originality–intrinsicality* our qualitative world acquires a logical *status*: it becomes intelligible in a sole center of intelligibility, in a rich unity, that forms the brief oasis of our intimate knowledge. This intelligibility is far from being absolute and complete, and it always meets new problems and difficulties, but it excludes the view according to which our world should be categorically defined as 'unintelligible,' 'irrational.' Others call mechanism 'rational' and 'intelligible,' and quality 'irrational.' How can abstract reason, which avoids what is most alive and intimate in our knowledge, and avoids, too, the source of any intelligibility relative to living reality, claim the monopoly of intelligibility? Sad pride of one who believes he can legitimate his ignorance, and assert his own superiority, denying thought.

Finally, it seems to me that we can never hope to understand the rise and development of intelligence and of value in biological evolution, except through the concept of being as essentially and *ab aeterno* an exigency. The determinate, as limit–concept, is not capable of intelligence, but only of exterior relations: intelligence arises in the play of the infinite and the finite, of potentiality and form, in the inexhaustible relation of conflict and solidarity between being and existing. And, if living nature is active potentiality, we may legitimately hold as likely, even apart from other considerations, that it is pervaded by intelligence.

V. THE ORIGINAL NODE AND ART

There are those who look for the nature of life in its rudimentary forms and those who look for it in its most explicit forms — in its reality, as it is said, "all unfolded." Philosophy rather follows this latter way, and therefore the philosopher is justified if he often turns importunately to art, drawn by his own problems. I would like here to consider some essential values of *poetic* thought and particularly of the work of art.

THE PERENNIAL FIRST. Poetic or artistic reality is a perennial *first*: not an *a tergo* causal process. Truly, the same should be said of all living reality, but there are differences of degree; for the extrinsic causal process has in it a part now more, now less relevant.

Extrinsic causality is always an interruption of authentic being. Being is origin; it is essentially, ultimately uncaused — not, however, to the extent that it does not bear within itself its cause. And the sense of origin often and intelligibly carries with it a sense of infinite origin, possible or necessary (intrinsically necessary).

There is a characteristic value of a work of art (not exclusively characteristic of it, but proper more generally to contemplative thought) that goes under various names, such as 'repose,' 'detachment,' 'balance.' A distinct value of serene calm intelligibly accompanies the high moment of creation, almost a divine suspense, a silence, a balance — which is not formal balance, symmetry, order, but something deeper and of another nature. This is the moment of infinite potentiality, radical, virgin of form; active potentiality still intact in its deep infinite: between one rhyme and another, between one voice and another. A pause of silent waiting, before the ineffable potency precipitates in the objectively determined existentiality that excludes it. Here the eternal *new* is present in all its uncompromised vastness; but not absolutely deprived of form, for if form did not already belong to it, it would not have that fullness of charm and that sense of unknown promise.

I say that this *first* is in poetry and in contemplation a moment that is felt as eternal because it is felt as an uncaused cause, one that must seemingly always be or always be able to return, exactly because it has its origin in itself, not in the past. Forgetful of the past, which is usually stubbornly determined to torment the present, almost detached from the past, song, in its fresh origin, is felt as eternal precisely because of this uncaused origin, this *first*.

The term 'detachment' reflects the same order of concepts. The artist identifies himself in an ardent originary causality that belongs to the most alive actuality of the present. And this originary causality tends to absorb all his personality and he finds in it his true freedom; but at the same time it counterbalances what remains in him of his separate self, and therefore it expresses a value of impersonality, of spiritual objectivity.

The secret of the value of that which, in absence of other terms, is described as 'repose,' 'tranquility,' 'serenity,' 'detachment,' lies, in my opinion, exactly in the power of an absolutely intrinsic characterization, not extrinsically caused, not derived.

THE NAKEDNESS OF THE IMMEDIATE ORIGIN. The *not-being-able-to-be-something-else* of poetic or artistic inspiration implies the active exclusion of a *being-able-to-be-something-else* or of a *being-able-not-to-be*. Otherwise the not-being-able-to-be-something-else will be mechanically necessitated, literally necessitated, either from the outside or from the inside. This active exclusion of something else may in a certain sense be ineluctable, but it will not have the character of literal necessity. Positivity rests on this point; through it intrinsic necessity is distinguished from literal necessity. And the purity and simplicity of the work of art depend on this positivity, which is intrinsic necessity, intrinsic finality or purposiveness, freedom, value. The more the artist is trammeled by forces acting *a retro*, the more his hand is moved by heavy extrinsic causality, or by extrinsic finality, the more will his work appear composite, devoid of the radical simplicity of the spirit.

The directness, the simplicity, the *nudity* of art come from an inner form that is ultimate positivity, creation; they come from the *nothing* that accompanies being and that is the measure, so to speak, or the other face of its positivity.

I repeat that simple perception, given that it be unity, is active potentiality, for only in the radical *posse* is there *unity*. It is therefore taken up in the center of thought, not as an element of construction, but as a participant in its nature. All the details constitute a single presence, an absolute presence, because in their reality of thought they are truly created by the thought and participate in its unity, and because this thought *is* unity — not indeed for reasons of contiguity or concomitance or as a means to an end among the various data, or some other thing, but, in the first place, because it is potentiality transparent to its own self, intuitive and constitutive space; and because of the sparking of radical kinships that belong to *poetic essence.*

A painting can make us sense, or rather touch with our hands, an ultimate, noncomposite reality. But this fontlike reality has no value or significance except in that it is integrity and spiritual concreteness, and it is a node of values implicit in thought's originality itself. Spontaneity, especially in art, means truth in this node of values.

I have endeavored to give examples of the radical relationships intelligibly implicit in the concept of originary causality — or, that is, of this creative spontaneity; but it will not be inopportune if here I draw attention to an example that has a particularly close relationship with art.

A value of universal intelligibility accompanies what is felt as intimate, and the more intimate it is the more does intelligibility accompany it: an intelligibility not confined to a determined country or century. Even in spite of cryptic poetry, symbolism, and other doctrines. What is felt as intimate is felt as universal, or, in a certain sense, as *eternal*. And it is in fact quite comprehensible that what is *originally creative* should at the same time have a value of intimacy and of powerfully *intrinsic* characterization. Here is, if I am not mistaken, the beginning of any philosophical deepening. But perhaps the value of intelligibility and eternity, proper to the most alive and distinct unicity of the act of thought, is in no field as relevant as it is in art. The value of a work of art is revealed mainly through its intimacy.

Represented images find their relationships more actively and deeply *ex principio*, matter gains spiritual lightness in the realm of an inner form through which — through which only — external reality is perceived, and which, though always necessary, can be now more, now less, prevalent, in certain respects, in comparison with material inertia. But the plasticity of inner form poses arduous problems. I hold that we must suppose, *as creation of thought*, an element of inertia, of exteriority, of resistance—a semiexistentiality X — capable of relation with physiological and physical conditions.

Such a semiexistentiality X corresponds in certain respects with what absolute idealism calls 'objective moment of thought' or thought that has been thought (rather than thought in the process of being thought), but it differs from it principally for the following reasons: (1) This semiexistentiality X does not pretend to resolve the problem of matter. That "matter may be nothing but thought" may be a remote conjecture. But that I, in the act of expressing myself, should be creating the physical medium I am using is something too absurd to dwell upon. The creation of X is not a creation of ordinary physical reality. (2) X belongs to the liveliest actuality of active thought no less than to thought in its abstract outlines or in its now more, now less passive forms. (3) Its character of inertia, of resistance, of exteriority, is assumed in order that there may be a common property through which psychic reality may come in contact with physiological and physical conditions. But the nature of this semimateriality remains an obscure problem.

How can these existents X be actual thought (psychic reality in general)? How can they be an integral part of the intimate unity of thought? The contact of existents does not *unite*. The radiant, centrifugal forces are, at least to a certain extent, understood. The forces of attraction, the gravitational forces and the forces of cohesion, remain obscure. The theory through which attraction would be explained as almost a countering push, a 'backward kick' to the radiant forces, seems to me, if I dare say so, desperate.[18]

For the existent to be a principle of real unity it has to be transformed into an infinite of itself, it has to be absorbed into the inner infinite — one and manyfold — of a radical *posse*: it has to be *deexistentialized*. This deexistentialization is indeed a constant delight of being, and it is known especially in love.

The concept of force (psychic and physical at the same time) can help us bring into evidence some difficulties and perhaps shed some light. Force (nonmechanical) is at the same time active potentiality — and existentiality. Thus in the force of a living creature the essentially undivided infinite (dynamic or of potency) and finite and divisible exteriority are united! And yet this exterior, finite, divisible, measurable reality is just what potentiality is not. On the one hand there is the accumulated physicochemical energy of the organism, necessitated according to processes of extrinsic causality; and on the other hand there is force in the psychic sense, or *power*, an undivided unity, analytically nothing.

It doesn't seem that the exterior or divisible element should be

---

[18] For "backward kick," see Viscount Samuel, *Essays in Physics* (Oxford: Blackwell, 1951), p. 97.

conceived as a façade or envelope: it penetrates all one's undivided strength. The living organism is loaded with inertial physicochemical forces, and these are transmuted — in a surprising way — into a force that is not mere force of inertia.

The concept of semimateriality, or 'subtle body,' of living reality, is found in innumerable traditions and doctrines, and various fields of research point to it: it deserves respect and deserves to be studied seriously. Now, in the plastic arts the problem of such a common ground between thought and material inertia presents itself as particularly evident. In a painting there is the coloring matter (physical reality, quantitatively measurable) and there is color (quality, thought) : there is in every trait the divisible and the undivided, the finite and the infinite, the existent and *being*. There is the intuitive and constitutive space — that is, the vision, not strictly localizable — and there is the objective space. How can we reconcile intuitive space, which cannot be measured, with objective space, which *is* measure? There is the painting-vision, and there is the existential substrate, determinate, measurable, of the coloring materials. But the painter sees no jump between the one thing and the other. He sees no jump between the psychic extension on the one hand, and on the other the material extension, that is, the crude multiplicity of the coexistent material elements. Is it perhaps because a principle of exteriority may not be germinally extraneous to the infinite of potency that makes the indivisibility of the act? And may it not already belong to the inwardness of thought, not only as a scheme of objective space, but as a reality of inertia created by thought itself?

The term 'creation' (and others derived from it or analogous to it) is much used, especially with reference to art, but in my judgment this term cannot be preserved except through the hypothesis of an existentiality X that is not physical reality: unless we are con-

tent in using the word lightly, as a vague, approximate, temporary — or falsely rhetorical — term. Naturally the concept of creation — that is, of a real and true positivity — meets with great
difficulties. I mention the following ones as most closely related to
the present paragraph. *Creation* implies creation of force, in contradiction to the law of conservation.[19] Moreover, how can these
resistances have with the physical a 'common ground' that is not
physical and that does not entirely share in the nature of physical
structure?[20]

QUALITY AS SUBSTANCE. According to the more common view,
reality is not in the *adjective* or *attribute*, but in the *noun* — often
an abstractly supposed existent. Art vindicates the reality of quality
in itself; in the same way poetry vindicates the reality of the adjective, or of the verb and the noun in their qualitative content.

Art vindicates and reveals quality as *substance*. For in art quality
does not need the prop of a determinate existent, but is alive with
a life of its own. In art, quality is ultimate reality, self-sustaining,
both through the originary value of self-actuation, and through the
inner infinite that is known as infinite feasibility and inner transparency. The finite of determinate existentiality is almost a crystal
urn that does not obscure that infinite, but which on the contrary is
lighted by it and transforms itself into active potentiality — that is,
into the *infinite of quality.* And a limpid word — one drawing its
intuitive content from radical values of the spirit rather than from
exterior experience — is a reality of origin, ultimately founded in
itself, not composite and not derivative, not provisional, not essentially referred to or leaning on something else: a bottomless and
shoreless substance, in the brief space of a lucid bud.

[19] See my *Philosophy of Potentiality*, pp. 24–26.
[20] Cf. *A Philosophy of Potentiality*, p. 22.

The proposition: "In order to do something, that is, in order to see, one must first be," expresses an obvious concept, but an exterior one, and is, ultimately, erroneous. Whoever says: "Someone sees," already removes himself from ontological reality; for the subject (active subject) of seeing is seeing itself! The mannequin we place before it or next to it represents nothing but extrinsic causality, which could never substitute for *seeing* — an originally active principle, a value of contact and actuation, *form* that is an originary potency of form.

And, as quality is not an attribute but a subject (active subject), similarly in art, quality is never an *object*. There exists nothing in the actuality of the work of art that is not living subjectivity and that may not be known through identification, therefore nothing that may rigorously be called an 'object' — if by 'object' we mean a distinct content of consciousness that opposes itself to a real agent–subject, or even something that exists independently of our thinking it. Form, in art, is not object: it is original value of actualization, *exigency* of form, active principle, motive-value. The *light* of freedom is not an object, but freedom itself in its profound eternity of origin and its inner transparency. It is the same with the light of creative spontaneity: every form of it is agent–subject and immediate sense of itself. Being as urge to be is immediately value. The false idea that the distinction between subject and object marks the beginning of consciousness has made of philosophy a sterile network of unilateral constructions, in an intellectualistic sense.

What I have said about quality, I must say about sensation — for instance, of the color red. In practice and in scientific observation sensation is generally an *instrument*, more or less imperfect, of knowing. But in contemplative thought it is felt, lived, as real in itself and not illusive or provisional.

Quality is never exactly comparable. The physical conditions of the color red, for instance, may be measured or compared and may be the main thing by far. But this red, in two places on the canvas, or in two different moments, cannot be demonstrated as being and cannot be presumed to be literally the same. And the more color is *active quality* — as, let us suppose, in Titian — the more will its force be unique and incomparable. And not because the personality of the artist *adds itself* to the color, but because he *identifies himself* with that color, because it already contains the key principle of his soul and of all that is created. The infinite of the soul is the same infinite that the loving texture of the instant is made of, and that already belongs to the *touch*, to the brush stroke, *and to sensation.*

When Pissarro, called in his time "the father of impressionism," talked of "free sensation," he expressed a truth of vast significance.[21] For sentient reality is always inner unity, and there is no inner unity except in freedom (that is, in potentiality in the active sense). And this is what we must admit inferentially, and also what we know, or seem to know, intimately and directly in sensibility, which gradually, without interruption, harmoniously lends itself to becoming an expression of every highest spiritual value, transparent interpreter and participant of value itself.

This is the secret of art: every least bit of sensible matter contains the rose of values ready to blossom in its splendor. "But what is there," one might ask, "in *sensation*, if you prick yourself with a pin? We admit there will be something well defined, and, on the other hand, something indefinite, and a strong sense of reality, and a germinal pluridimensionality, not only on the surface. Your sensation, we admit, will exceed the distinct sensory organ. We might

---

[21] Camille Pissarro, *Lettres à son fils Lucien*: "Mais il faut . . . des sensations *libres*, dégagées de toute autre chose que sa propre sensation" (Paris: Michel, 1950), p. 291; cf. pp. 330, 343.

even recognize in it an intrinsic, originary nature . . . but we are a long way from the sentiment of charity and from the visions of art!" I reply, certainly the universal ethic does not arise unless the consciousness of a common essence issues forth in the contrast among creatures; certainly conditions and determining causes are necessary . . . But first of all we should be surprised not by how much a rudimentary sensation already contains, but by its not containing yet more. We should marvel that since it is activity, subjectivity, unity, quality, it should not be the key principle of other values besides. And I repeat that it is artificial and naive to try to explain actual reality, starting with insignificant elements (in this case raw sensation), by having recourse to numerous additions, or new categories in which the problem of origins is eluded. Without doubt the present is enriched by the past, is enriched by all the specifications and integrations of the biological past. But the tendency is to consider unilaterally the explicative value of the determining conditions.

And I don't deny, concerning the value of sensation, that one of the dominant aspirations in the history of civilization is, or ought to be, that of elevating oneself from a low sensuality to a purer spirituality. But here the problem is a different one, and we must beware of embracing a false spirituality.

The distinction among sense, sentiment, and thought is — to my mind, and despite the authority of James — mistakenly considered as fundamental; nor does one truly meet with it in reality! The radical distinction is that between thought instrumentally conceived, and thought that is essentially and undividedly sense, originary value, intimate and contemplative knowledge.

FORM AND REALIZATION. The word 'realize,' in art, though it sounds harsh, and though it is, in this usage, a gallicism, expresses with some advantage what may also be expressed by the terms 'actuate' and 'create.' It expresses the same concept as the word 'form,' understood in its active meaning of *formative principle.* As compared with 'create,' it has less need of clarification, and at the same time it contains all the problems of the concept of creativity. In the first place it implies the idea of a unity issuing from the source, immediate, born with the act: an intimate, absolute unity, an undivided and direct presence. *Form* primarily consists in the simplicity of self-realization.

Even in an art that endeavors only to be a mere reproduction of objective reality, *realization*, a modest term, implies the spirit, its profoundest values.

'To realize' may mean to make something sensibly present and unequivocally recognizable. It may mean to give sensible form (in a symbol) to something that otherwise would be only abstractly conceivable. But even without extrinsic references, realization in art is already an expression–revelation of the spirit: expression, for example, of a unity of the finite and the infinite, of conditionality and originality–intrinsicality, found in any material sign insofar as it is a lively reality of thought. And in this connection let me finally remark that whoever says that art is the realm of the finite is expressing himself in a most improper way. In the first place the *unique* and the *unequivocal* (to which perhaps he is referring) are altogether different from the finite: the finite is actually what is comparable. But, above all, form in its very concreteness and sensible evidence profoundly implies the discovery of essential kinships of the spirit; and it is not opposed to the universal, that is, to the value of universality, or eternity — which is as concrete a thing as anything else ever can be — but rather to generalities and to exterior constructions, to anything that is not *created*.

CHAPTER 3

The Immediate Corporeity of Thought

An analysis of the doctrines concerning the relationship or the difficulty in the relationship between psychic reality and physical reality would require volumes. There are those that recognize an efficacious interrelation between psychic reality and matter or physical energy, and those that definitely exclude it (materialistic monism, idealistic monism, psychophysiological parallelism, theory of twofold access or twofold knowledge of an identical reality ...).

It seems to me that today there is a tendency — particularly in the fields of neurology, psychoneurology, and psychiatry — to pass over the difference between the psychic and the physical. On my part I hold that the student who wants to try to resolve the problem of the relation between the psyche on the one hand and matter or physical energy on the other must stress the apparent antinomy between them, and first express his thoughts about the nature of psychic reality. I shall therefore summarize some things I have said elsewhere, and I hope the reader will forgive my assertive manner, perhaps inevitable in a kind of compendium.[1]

[1] Cf. *A Philosophy of Potentiality* and chapter 2 of this volume.

Being (subjective) is an ever-originary exigency or urge. I am not saying "urge to be," for that would be equivalent to giving again to 'being' the status of an object, a given and obscure reality; and at the same time the term 'exigency' would be deprived of its content. Being as exigency, as an ever-originary urge — implies, intelligibly, intrinsic purposiveness or finality. It implies ontological newness, that is, creativity. It equally means unicity, unrepeatability, singularity. It contains the principle of individuality. It is undivided psychic *presence*, actually felt and experienced potentiality: only in the concept of potentiality are the one and the manifold intelligibly a single reality. Being as exigency therefore presents an intimate characterization, not determined by given conditions or ideas or rules or laws, but born ever anew according to the intrinsic nature of an actual origin. This potent intrinsicality of characterization is in itself an originary value of infinity, of universality — which, however, does not necessarily imply a universal validity of fact. *Being*, in each of its intense moments, is essence — the implicit sense of its profound intrinsicality of nature.

The *finite* — the objectively determined — isn't the touchstone of reality. Thought in its abstract constructions wants the finite, the measurable, the divisible; but it always returns to the undivided as to its true, ultimate reality, that is, to active potentiality, which is essentially undivided. The inner subjective infinite is a primary reality. The greatest value — and force — of the infinite isn't in the urge to surpass the given limit; it isn't in the formal implication of the concept of the finite — which without something beyond itself cannot be represented or conceived; it isn't in the objective infinite (in the astronomical infinite, the infinitely small, the mathematical infinite); it isn't even in the intimate infinity of the *posse*, of *potentiality*, of its essentially inapprehensible and imperceptible graduality, dynamically intended. These motive-values are indeed the infinite's own, but they are not its strongest reality. The core of the infinite is in the supremely *intrinsic* characterization of the ontological new, through which this core is felt as an infinite necessity–possibility, as a value of universality or eternity, and, at the same point, as originality, as freedom. Life is all in the inner infinite of subjective being. The creature that dies falls from the infinite into the *finite*, devoid of subjectivity and of potentiality. The inner infinite — absolutely unobjectifiable, irreducible to objectively determined data — is a primal, supreme reality; from it is born the idea or the sense of a limit, and not vice versa.

I use the word 'determinate' in the sense of objectively determinate, given, finite, devoid of potentiality, of subjectivity, of real activity; divisible, numerable. The same term, it is understood, is also used with reference to thought, but in quite a different sense. 'Determinate' and 'determinacy,' with reference to the activity of thought and of the psyche in general, can mean singularity, distinctness, precision, irrevocability, unequivocability, and so forth. But in this use of the terms we shall be very remote from the exactly, literally 'determinate' of the mechanistic conception. For even in the most arid thought constructed upon given elements, any moment, or point, does not constitute a psychic presence unless it is made an infinite of itself, a principle of interpretation and limitless transparency, a moment of comprehension without definite limits. The *finite* of thought is always, in every moment, an infinite of itself and a term *ad quem*. The point, as reality of thought or psychic reality, is quite intelligible to us, intelligible in a relationship of inseparable values, bound to the positivity of being. We can say that it is *powerfully, potently* determinate, precise, distinct: but in that adverb 'powerfully' there is hidden the infinite of indeterminacy. The physical 'point,' on the other hand, is a hopelessly obscure concept. For we know that the concepts of contiguity, the continuous, the discontinuous, divisibility, the infinitely small, are concepts that are full of difficulties if we keep to our own scheme of matter, and even more so if we question without bias physical reality itself.

Contrary to dominant opinion, the finite is less intelligible or less rational than the infinite; divisibility (and measurability) is less intelligible than the undivided — if we start from the inner experience of doing, of value, of love, of hate, or of any psychic reality, in fact, of all the vocabulary of the spirit.

In order perhaps to gloss over or to hide the gap between psychic reality and physical reality, there is a widespread tendency to represent sensation as almost a no-man's-land, a negligible reality, one presenting few problems. The neurologist will lightly say that the last thing to happen in a neurophysiological process 'generates' sensation — almost as if this were a small thing. But sensation is already subjectivity, is already undivided presence against the multiplicity that we suppose is inherent in physiological conditions and stimuli. There is no doubt that in the interpretation of external reality, sensation may be fallible and deceptive; but it is in itself already a quality and it lends itself to the expression of the highest values, apparently without discontinuity, without the intervention of archetypal ideas or of categories; it is or it becomes quality in the full value and force of the word, an infinite of itself, a presence, or inner transparency, or relief, or 'dimension' or psychic depth.

Even the most passive of sensations, in order to be an undivided whole — essentially undivided — must participate in the nature of the *posse*; that is, it must be originally active, and not inertia; and similarly it must be active in order to have an efficient relation with its own physiological reality, if we admit that it is distinct from it. The act of unification of the multiple is not subsequent to sensation or distinct from it. The contention that sensation needs to be given a form and is in itself formless is a radical error.

Deriving thought from sensation, in certain forms of sensism, or *constructing* it, starting from sensation, with the addition of categories, means ignoring the common nature of sensibility and of true reason; and this common nature, or ever-originally operative principle, is incomparably the principal thing. Sensation is already value — I mean originary value, not conventional or instrumental. The least glow of sensibility is already a revelation of an immense reality that underlies the living world and is in fact opposed to mechanism.

In a recent work, Herbert Feigl tentatively presents the thesis that there is an absolute identity between the psychic fact and the neurophysiological fact,[2] even though he admits the causal efficacy of psychic reality over physiological reality, and vice versa (inter-actionism)[3] — and, to tell the truth, I don't understand how this is compatible with the thesis of a perfect identity. He imagines that in future centuries, with the advances in psycho-neurophysiology, with the help of an autoencephaloscope a trained person will be able to see projected on a screen the physiological phenomena, and feel within himself at the same time the related states of mind, the sensations and shades of sensations.[4] This does not mean a great deal, since no one excludes that, for instance, one may virtually recognize in the macrophysics or in the microphysics of musical chords a piece of music that one also hears. The difficulty lies in

[2] "The 'Mental' and the 'Physical'," in H. Feigl *et al.*, eds., *Concepts, Theories, and the Mind–Body Problem*, Minnesota Studies in the Philosophy of Science, vol. 2 (Minneapolis: University of Minnesota Press, 1958), pp. 370–497.

[3] Ibid., p. 474 and passim.

[4] Ibid., p. 456; cf. pp. 430, 473–74.

the relation between the psychic presence and its physiological conditions. The author pauses on this difficulty only briefly;[5] he holds that it can be surmounted because, he says, models can be devised (and something of this kind has been done) that, for example, would let us reduce the enormous physiological complication and multiplicity to a sort of punctuality and to the unity of a psychical moment — and other *models* with reference to other supposed antinomies or disparities. But these models are constructed on the presupposition that there is no reality other than one constituted of objectively determinate data, and they do not seem to lead to anything that may be conceived as subjective reality.

The crucial point in the problem of the relation between the psyche and the body lies in how an analytically inapprehensible qualitative reality can have contact with an objectively given and measurable quantitative reality.

My assumption is that thought may be immediately force. I mean 'thought' in the broad sense: psychic reality, subjectivity in general. That psychic reality may be also *force*, immediately, essentially, is a fairly common conviction; but the term 'force' has various meanings.

There is a force I would call *consubstantial* with thought that has various names: intimate, living, whole, undivided, creative, originary, lyrical, luminous, plastic force; virgin force, flexible force; active, subjective, substantial, nonmechanical force; and also intrinsically tendential, intentional, final or purposive force. One refers to it or describes it with numberless expressions, such as 'force of attention,' 'the force of one's will or willpower,' 'force of expression,' the 'force' of a color, 'the force of passion,' 'the force of love,'

[5] Ibid., p. 458.

'force of spirit,' 'force of faith,' 'formative force,' and so on.

In these expressions we generally intend a psychophysiological force (and we stress its psychic, mental aspect). Or at times we mean to describe a psychic, pure, primary, 'hyperorganic' force.[6]

Especially in an effort, force is felt as force, or rather as creation of force. Sometimes, on the other hand, it is not felt as such, but it must (I maintain) be necessarily admitted as a condition of efficient relation between the psychic and the physiological. In all these usages, the term 'force' is not simply a generic collective name, for it always implies a certain idea of extrinsic causality, and, at the same time, of originality; that is, of a not absolutely derivative force.

I hold that an intimate force is essential to the positivity of the subjective being. Positivity cannot be understood without a negative possibility, even if it is condemned never to prevail; should the negative possibility cease we would have inert form, mere mechanism, nothing psychic. Any affirmation — and even a denial is, in a sense, an affirmation — confirms this positivity, and implies a negative possibility — not factual, but in the thought of the person who thinks it and of the person to whom the affirmation is directed. The affirmation will be, in many respects, limited, but its reality of thought consists in its being an infinite of itself against numberless possible oppositions (objections, doubts, contradictions, difficulties, more or less radical or insistent negations); and therefore it is also — I apologize for mentioning the obvious — a moment of intimate force.

The triangle in the abstract is neither right-angled nor equilateral nor anything else: the idea of a triangle resolves itself in forces or tendencies. Recognizing a person also does not require

---

[6] Maine de Biran, *Journal* (Neuchâtel: Editions de la Baconnière, 1957), 3: 35; also *Oeuvres Choisies* (Paris: Aubier, 1942), pp. 32, 69.

exact coincidence: the memory of the person resolves itself in forces or tendencies. Any memory, either of a person or a thing, presents in our minds a reality of tendentiality. Nor can one hold that these *thinking* forces, intrinsically purposive forces or tendencies, should primarily be realities of atoms, of protons and electrons. They seem to have to be creative, autocreative, free forces, and at the same time physically efficacious, capable of being *turned into* an energy objectively determined (within the limits of physical determinism) and measurable.

We must admit in the subconscious the existence of a vast halo of matter that has already become quality — and intelligence — that rushes to bring us words, to fill gaps, to correct errors, not only according to relations of concomitance and contiguity of facts, but also according to conceptual affinities — discovery of relationships in the originary node of values, summoning of assonances and rhymes, and so forth: qualitative, living realities that cannot but be force.

The truths of essence are, perhaps, the greatest force — even though George Santayana, with amiable lightness, asserts the ineffectuality of essences. The essence of the universal ethic does not lie in a formal universality, but in an ever-unsatisfied charity. Charity is consciousness, or *discovery*, of an infinite identity of essence among creatures. This inner infinite belongs to the ultimate reality of being as an underivable positivity and as a deep intrinsic characterization of this same positivity. The horror one experiences when confronted by cruelty testifies to the force of the eternal in sensitive pity. (By 'eternal' I mean always the powerful intrinsicality of character of the ontological new, not an eternity of fact that we do not know.)

Words, fundamentally, are not symbols, nor conventions, nor

instruments, but reality — naked, ultimate — of the spirit;[7] and they are ever *new*. They are identically spirit and body. By 'body' I don't mean properly matter, but matter insofar as it is transformed into qualitative reality. Any sound actually heard or imagined is subjectivity, value, force, presence; and the dominant personality identifies itself in it, because it shares the same profound qualitative substance.

In the same way color (not the coloring matter) is for the painter identically spirit and body, unicity, value of intimacy and intrinsicality, of impersonality, free joy, color that sings, transparency or infinite presence of itself, beyond the distinction between subject and object; cognitive value, where knowing is being. Quality, in a practical respect, can be a mere connotation, but for the artist it is ultimate, absolute reality; and such it truly is, in the ontological sense *a parte subjecti*. It is intimate force and, in a certain sense, it is body — not physical. Therefore the painter, indeed in the mere brushstroke, has faith that he is involved in a profound reality, luminous and causal at the same time.

"The true artist" (as I have said) is "matter inspirited";[8] but by 'matter' I don't here mean physical reality precisely, but rather a matter–quality ('matter of expression') that already contains germinally the node of values, and that lights itself with all the light of the spirit — that is, with a relationship of values bound to a radical, underived positivity of being (subjective). This matter–quality is thought, I assume, in its aspect of force–resistance, which it unfolds with particular richness as it comes in contact with physical reality, which it generally needs.

---

[7] Cf. my *English Poetry and Its Contribution to the Knowledge of a Creative Principle*, pp. 150–51, 172.

[8] *Intelligence in Expression*, p. 17.

We always see things through this living and substantial force, ultimately characterized by its own underived positivity, and modulated, modified, specified by physiological conditions and stimuli.

The substance of sounds *a parte subjecti* is this same reality: forces longing to integrate and renew themselves in a sole source.

We see and feel everything in a 'corporeity'—or substantiality—not measurable by an instrument, at the same time qualitative and causal.

If I see the green of a leaf, what is the ultimate reality of that green? Not my physiological conditions, nor external conditions — things that have no *color* — but an originary force, certainly modulated and in a certain sense determined by neurophysiological conditions, by external stimuli, and by thousandfold millenary experiences — but not constituted by these.

Corporeity and thought are antithetical terms, since 'body' means primarily limit, an objectively given and measurable reality. If, however, I use the term 'corporeity' (for example, here to indicate the force of color), that is because this same word can also suggest the idea of substance in two respects: (1) something that is originally self-sustaining, not absolutely derived and inert substance; moment of intrinsic finality, not decomposable, not reducible to existent data; originary, unitary, creative force, whose lifeline is an element of true positivity; and (2) a principle of extrinsic causality, which implies some form of resistance.

If one can speak of creation in any respect, and especially with reference to the activity of thought, one should also be able to speak of creation of intimate force, for this is exactly co-essential with every creation of thought — with every vision, with every perception — and couldn't *not* share in its unitary and creative nature. But all this presupposes that the terms 'creation,' 'creativity,' can and should be taken seriously and used in their full ontological significance.[9]

The term 'creation' is used by scientists with a certain ease denied philosophers, and not only in a provisional or metaphorical way. Fred Hoyle writes,

This is, perhaps, the most surprising of all the conceptions described in this book. For I find myself forced to assume that the nature of the Universe requires continuous creation — the perpetual bringing into being of new background material. . . . The most obvious question to ask about continuous creation is this: Where does the created material come from? It comes from nowhere. Matter simply appears, is created. At one time created atoms do not exist, and at a later time they do. . . . This may seem a very strange idea and I agree that it is, but in science it does not matter how strange an idea may seem so long as it works — that is to say, so long as the idea can be expressed in a precise form, and so long as its consequences are found to be in agreement with observation.[10]

Is the continuous origin of being as an urge or exigency perhaps more unlikely than the continuous origin of matter–energy? I must note, however, that a continuous origin of being as an exigency means a continuous origin of value — and this represents a more arduous problem.

Determinism is not demonstrated by experience, but it imposes itself on the human mind through a generally implicit form of reasoning, which is also a sophism: What does not exist can do nothing, and especially cannot create itself; and what exists has no need of being created. Opposed to this is the inanity of an all-derived uni-

[9] I use the word 'creativity' in order to avoid the equivocation of a creation *ab extra*: see chapter 2 of this volume, under "The Rose of Values."

[10] Fred Hoyle, *The Nature of the Universe* (New York: Penguin Books, 1951), pp. 109–110.

verse, and the consideration that the concept of an actual, intrinsically characterized origin — self-becoming, self-creation, originality, spontaneity, the idea of something really *active* — arises everywhere in the study of aesthetic, ethical, logical problems, especially
in the contrast with false and clumsy derivationist solutions. Concerning the reasoning just mentioned, one should observe that substantial positivity cannot be split into (1) an already existing subject that creates, *ab extra*, (2) something positive — that would not
be entirely positive any more, but derivative. One should consider
the concept of a really active positivity pitted against an absolutely inherent negativity or passivity; this positivity is not mere
chance (which would comprise nothing psychic or mental), and it
owes to its own nature of underived positivity its intrinsic and rich
characterization.[11]

But the greatest obstacle we encounter lies in creativity, once
it is recognized as ultimate reality, upsetting the traditional concept of *substance*. I mean the concept according to which substance
is what remains identical throughout change. Certainly mere conservation — mere derivation — is not substance. But also the concept of substance as underived, unconditional, subsisting by and for
itself, admits or can admit, it seems to me, the idea of substance as
static reality.

---

[11] In extreme hypothesis, it must be said that even if in indeterminacy
there should be concealed a strictly exact measure, of which we were essentially unaware, indeterminacy would nevertheless always be a *reality of illusion*, from which all of life — the very origin of life — depends. The fact
that someone may, without being conscious of it, obey another will (e.g., of
a hypnotist) or form-type, does not affect the ontological problem of freedom. Determinacy is one thing, predetermination, or destiny, or fate, quite
another. (Cf. my book *Studi sulle precognizioni* and my article "Il Nuovo
ontologico e i Fenomeni precognitivi," in *Il Giornale Italiano per la Ricerca
Psichica*, vols. 1–3 (1964).

Substance, to my way of thinking, is what sustains itself originally: a power creative in itself, ever new, and therefore also ever fleeting; intrinsically and perpetually characterized by its own underived positivity. Thought must be said to be 'substance' because it is originally self-sustaining — and because it is essentially undivided reality, not reducible into elements, and, moreover, because it has *at the same time* causal efficacy. For the concept of permanence as conservation, as literal identity–immutability, as immobility, as extra-temporality, we must substitute the concept of constancy — constancy in the intimate and rich characterization of being as underivable positivity. The permanence and, in a sense, the immutability of substance is in reality a continuous new. Nothing is more absurd than setting up principles and *ideas* as immobile realities in order to explain and bear witness to value and spirit!

Then there is a difficulty that concerns us more directly. This creativity belongs to a mental order — and total derivation and automatism would exclude it. But intimate, lived, creative force produces (we know not how) mechanical force, and this, as far as we know, is wholly derived and obeys the law of conservation. Shall we say that our intimate effort adds reality to the physical universe?

Experiments have been made from which it was seen that the potential energy introduced into a living organism with its ingested food corresponded to the kinetic energy produced.[12] One might object that these experiments should be repeated today, when the law of conservation and noncreation of energy is no more a dogma. But above all, even if an excess of force (not referable to the calories introduced with the food) were never to result, it nevertheless has not been demonstrated nor is it evident, it seems to me, that force

[12] See my *Philosophy of Potentiality*, p. 25.

created, and perhaps all expended in exploiting and exhausting the potential energy of the organism, should be accounted for by the kinetic energy produced.

We must ask ourselves if the relation between intimate reality and the physiological element would not be more understandable if we admitted in physical matter–energy a principle of subjectivity, according to a panpsychistic conception, or idealistic monism, against any dualism or pluralism.

But as a matter of fact we see no sign of subjectivity in physical reality. There are arguments in this sense, that is in the sense of a monism of a mental or psychic order; but these arguments seem to me to remain too conjectural and indirect. I shall recall some of them.

1. In physical reality we are faced with irreducible properties and indivisible quantities. Though for millennia the indivisibility of the ultimate elements of matter has been considered something intelligible *par excellence*, the undivided in regard to matter nevertheless remains an enigma; the undivided is intelligible to us only in the analogy of the verb *can*. In the physics of the discontinuous one does not understand what it is that places a limit on the divisibility of the inert. The stability of elementary particles not only engages formidable energies, but, more generally, the conservation of something as such is certainly not an obvious thing, nor does it fit in with our naive schemes about matter. The ultimate properties of matter make us suspect the existence of intrinsically founded ties: not only necessity of derivation, relation, conditionality, but intrinsic necessities. We can accept with suspended judgment these intrinsic necessities — referable not to determining, but to constitutive causes: if, however, we insist on reflecting upon their possible

intimate nature, it seems necessary to resort to the concept of a force or urge that relies on itself, and therefore on something intrinsically final or purposive — and this would lead us back to a mental or psychic order (however remote from us).

2. Physicists demonstrate an 'essential' indeterminism due to the disturbances that observation cannot but bring on observed phenomena; but they are not explicit about whether this essential indeterminism of the phenomena concerns also the reality, quite independent of our observation of them, that statistical knowledge seems to imply. Physical indeterminism, therefore, does open the way to the possibility of an indeterminism that is an ultimate reality in the field of physics, but it does not demonstrate it. On the other hand, *chance*, to which we are referring, belongs to the world of objectively determined data and does not seem to have any affinity with psychic indeterminacy, which is potentiality, an actual value of the infinite. There are those who associate the concept of chance with the concept of tendency or tension. But *tension* (or tendency) can be understood in the mechanical sense — as with any other necessity in a mechanical system. If, on the other hand, tension is understood as psychic reality, that is, subjective tension, then it implies a sense of direction — in the undivided — and therefore plurality in the unity of a *presence*, of which we see no trace in physical phenomena.

3. The idea that in being there may be a deep positivity coextensive with the universe: the unlikelihood that this immense underivable positivity should not occupy the universe, and, as Emily Brontë says, "every existence" — "Though earth and man were gone." [13]

[13] Emily Brontë, "No coward soul is mine . . . ."

4. The leveling off of energy induces one to conjecture that there is a source without which everything would reduce itself, or would already have been reduced, to nothing. Creativity or subjectivity could be this source, but it clearly would be wholly inadequate were it confined to life in its obvious forms and were it not inherent in matter–energy.

5. The greater simplicity of one reality. Dualism makes two-fold the problem of first origins — if ever first origins existed.

I shall not dwell on the subject; I will say in conclusion that if in microphysics there is an originally active principle, it eludes us.[14] In any case the problem with which we are particularly concerned, that is, that of the relation between thought and its physical expression, is probably contained in the problem of the relation between thought and matter–energy considered only in its reality of mass.

The psychic reality that we ordinarily know is already always psycho-neurophysiological reality. Now the problem that concerns us lies in the relation between the neurophysiological conditions on the one hand and a *primary* psychic reality, distinct in every way, on the other. It will be pointed out that if what is psychic does not exist without physiological conditions, then we shall not understand what this psychic reality, which we want to oppose to physiological conditions, can be. And yet, as long as psychology isn't reduced to physiology, what is psychic must clearly have a reality of its own. And, as I firmly maintain, in order for it to have a relation with physiological conditions—whether to exercise effective action upon

---

[14] Cf., however, in a less contrary sense, Raymond Ruyer, *Néo-finalisme* (Paris: Presses Universitaires de France, 1952), pp. 155 *et seq.*

them, or to be subjected to them — what is psychic must have a force of its own.

The existence of a primary psychic reality, 'pure,' direct, and not psycho-neurophysiological, is another question. One cannot but call attention at this point to organisms that are not provided with nervous systems, and that, to all appearances, behave not in a blindly derivative way, not mechanically. And Raymond Ruyer observes from a histological viewpoint that a comparison between a nerve cell and any other cell of an organism does not justify the assumption that subjectivity begins only with the nerve cell.[15] We must, then, ask ourselves if in superior organisms a direct conscience-force does not sometimes intervene to integrate and also to substitute for the ordinary neurophysiological processes, in which, as it seems, life is channeled and attains a greater efficiency and richness, but without which it would be condemned to perish.

Even parapsychological phenomena, such as telekinetic phenomena, do not indicate whether in a particular case the effect is produced by physical forces (for example, 'unknown vibrations'), in turn produced by the psycho-physiological force of the medium or others; whether it is due to the transference of psycho-physiological centers; or whether it should be attributed to a primary psychic reality capable of forming itself in a certain density and resistance (without, however, losing its mental character, its character of a unitary and, to a certain degree, intelligent force); or to a concourse of these forces.

Sometimes in everyday life and in art we are aware of an inner form of such simplicity and integrity that physiological processes do not by themselves seem capable of constituting an adequate

[15] *Eléments de psycho-biologie* (Paris: Presses Universitaires de France, 1946), p. 29.

medium for its expression. Thus, for example, when on the stage the modest face of an actress lights up and is transfigured, surprising us with its beauty. Nor is it different in the case of the stigmata — phenomena that belong to the preternatural and have an affinity with materializations, disintegrations, objective hallucinations, and other categories of parapsychological phenomena. Once we exclude the possibility of discovering their explanation in ordinary neurophysiological processes, we can't understand how the inner vision could suddenly find — much less create — the suitable, objectively existent, photographable, physical material.

Similarly, the 'spiritual body' ($\sigma\hat{\omega}\mu\alpha$ $\pi\nu\epsilon\upsilon\mu\alpha\tau\iota\kappa\acute{o}\nu$) of the religious tradition can leave unsolved or not touch at all the problem of the relation between spirit and matter, and simply imply a *more subtle* matter (or physical energy) than the one we know.

It is useless to try to find an element intermediate between the psychic and the physical. Whatever least remnant of organic or inorganic matter thought should use, it would always be matter, or physical energy, and the problem that concerns us would only be shifted and remain unsolved. If subjectivity is not, as it most surely isn't, an epiphenomenon, it must be force *ab initio*, or it shall never be. And this originary force of being as urge, as exigency, intimately undivided and causal at the same time, active, creative, protected from the reversibility and relativity of movement, cannot be the matter–energy of the physicists.

It is not physical reality, in the first place, because we cannot believe that we can create, in the act of thinking, matter–energy made of molecules, atoms, electrons, positrons, cohesive forces, and so forth. On the other hand, this activity that ever renews itself, actual positivity–infinity, indivisible, bears no resemblance to the objectively determined and given, blind, calculable forces of mere

conservation. Further, as I assume, it is the substance of our representations, and it seems to me that its immediate expressive ade-
quacy would hardly be conceivable if it were rigid matter–energy:
the originary plasma follows the delicate blendings of the light and
shade of thought because it *is* these blendings, because it *is* thought.
There can be no discontinuity between the psyche and its intimate,
inherent creative force. Such a native force of thought is finally an
aspect of its positivity.

Naturally, let it be said in parenthesis, I don't mean to exalt the
forceful aspect of the psyche. Force tends to represent spirit in its
extrinsic causality; and when it serves superior values one is not
aware of it in itself. And I know that obsequiousness to force is
peculiar to coward souls. But this has little to do with the problem
of conscience-force — taken as terms that cannot be sundered.

I shall not return to the argument of minimal devices capable of
liberating accumulated physical energies. In the first place, the
problem of the relation between the psychic force that is engaged
(though it be very small) and the material means (though they be
very ingenious) would not be solved. But above all, ordinary experience suggests rather psycho-physiological forces that are propor-
tionate to the effects. It is much more likely that intimate force
engages, so to speak, all its power in its relations with neuromuscu-
lar currents, in a process (whatever that may be) bent on producing
variations of inert movement of external bodies.

The living and substantial, true, originally active force of which
I speak is (it is well to stress it) quite a different concept from that
of 'force' as a temporary name in mathematical-functional conceptions, or as a superfluous name that, according to many scientists,
should be eliminated from physical science. Now this intimate
force that concerns us could never exercise its action upon physiological conditions, for example, upon neuro-electrical currents

whose engrams are recorded, if it did not possess in itself something like *resistance* (or, by other names, a certain relative impenetrability, externality, compactness, consistency). Nor could the resistance that we must suppose be a superficial or marginal reality: it must be a free, undivided force coextensive with quality itself. There would have to be a 'point of contact,' a 'meeting,' a 'hold,' an 'application' . . . all provisional and obscure terms. And at the same time this resistance would always have to be subjectivity, sensibility; it would always have to retain its originary unity, its character of presence, the absolutely intrinsic purposiveness of the urge to be; it could not fall into the objectively determined, inert, dead, divisible existent. And this would have to happen precisely at the moment in which this same unitary force makes its incisive mark on physical processes. But how could this resistance impress, or be subjected to, matter without sharing its nature?

And yet it seems that this must in fact be so. Contact with matter does not lend materiality to perception. Contact, whether in opposition to or in support of physiological conditions, does not give materiality to psychic reality. For instance, coloring matter (physical reality) does not reduce the force of color to a merely derivative, quantitative reality or to inert movement. And yet who will deny a contact, whatever it may be, between coloring matter and *color* (quality)? We have, on matter's side, luminiferous wave-corpuscles that are neither light nor color, neuro-electrical currents, chemical compounds, and so forth. And now these same *colors* are intimate force, are a moment of internal transparency, that is, of accurate presence, are an infinite self-identity overwhelming the material multiplicity of determinate and measurable existents, are quality–substance.

But we are always at the same point. How can we conceive of this resistance as not being physical and yet as being physically efficacious? Will intimate, living force exercise its action upon the same point at which it adapts itself to a finite, divisible, inert reality? Will effort have to fix itself, transform itself into an objectively determinate and given existent (or group of existents), and so lose its inner infinity and potentiality and its unitary nature first where it is, and should be, most really itself?

Perhaps in the case of effort the relationship between quality and quantity can be touched at closer range. The dynamometer indicates a quantitative reality, but does not portray effort. In a world of objectively determinate existents, where the infinite of *possibilities* urgent in the act is lacking, there is no need for effort. The *more and the less* of effort is its *raison d'être*, a motive value, a qualitative reality. And propping effort or tension next to a determinate and given subject is a mistake: its cause and its reality lie in the liveliest actuality of tension itself, in an essential uncertainty that is not an *accident*, but substance . . .

This does not clear up the difficulty advanced. It merits pointing out, however, that the *opacity* of effort — the fact that wherever the extrinsic causal action is keener, activity tends to lose its luminosity and spirituality — perhaps reflects or indicates or confirms something absolutely real in the intimate formation of a resistance in the ambit of the psyche and at the expense of some values of the psyche itself.

The mode or way of the efficacious relation between intimate force and physiological reality isn't at all clear: but the impossibility of this relation is also neither clear nor ultimately demonstrated. And why is it, if such an impossibility really exists, that in all of living nature the psyche longs for matter, potentiates itself in it, enriches and refines itself in it? Material inertia evidently doesn't contaminate free force, but rather excites it. Contact with matter, material actualization, is a motive-value. Nor is it demonstrated that in its contact with matter, intimate force must share its nature in order to act or be acted upon by matter itself: it isn't demonstrated that the *posse* is incapable of exerting itself on matter and particularly on physiological conditions — except through the assumption of the properties of inert conservation, of divisibility, and others that describe matter in its reality of mass. Every relation implies a common element: but is this necessity for a homogeneous *quid* a simple and univocal concept?

We feel that our effort doesn't cease to be undivided and originally active even in material contact; the solidity of matter doesn't solidify effort; it leaves intact the reality of tension (tension of a mental kind).

It seems that originary force itself must rebel against anything whose concentration or resistance or consistency or precise determinacy might turn it into something dead.

And we must also say, without fear of discrediting ourselves: Is it possible that intimate force *won't* find a way to produce movement? For the thirst for its materialization is everywhere in life, and we are ever more cognizant that life is teeming with inventions in pursuing what are apparently its intentions.

We are so much in the dark as to the nature of this intimate lived force, and so much the more as to the intimate and ultimate reality of physical forces, that we cannot, on the basis of the apparent antinomy, reject with the simplistic manner and smugness of sophists either the one or the other. If anything, we should blame our schemes and remember that humility is the supreme foundation of scientific objectivity.

To my mind, the only way to try to solve the problem that concerns us is to admit this efficacious interrelationship and to study more deeply the nature of an intimate, immediate force of thought and the nature of psychic reality in general. It seems to me that we must keep to these main points and: (1) clarify our concept of subjectivity and stress the apparent antinomy; (2) admit an efficacious reciprocal action; (3) recognize a nonphysical force absolutely consubstantial with thought, with subjectivity; and (4), above all, penetrate more deeply into the nature of this force.

The concept of force is always to be found in philosophy, now in the significance of causality, now as a principle (for example, *vis vitae, vis medicatrix naturae*). But, unless I err, there is a lack of specific studies on the concept of intimate force in relation to value, and, at the same time, in relation to mechanical and physical force.[16]

---

[16] For the concept of force, especially with reference to physics, cf. Max Jammer, *Concepts of Force: A Study in the Foundations of Dynamics* (Cambridge: Harvard University Press, 1957).

CHAPTER 4

Difficulties with the Concept of the Underived Active

I would here like to consider particularly some difficulties with the concept of psychological indeterminacy.

I have said elsewhere that the subjective being, in whatever way provoked or necessitated, *inasmuch as it is*, is originary activity, true positivity.[1] One can object that *inasmuch as it is not* it has no power, and much less can it be *causa sui*; and since this 'new' of active non-predeterminacy, the ontological, creative new, is a continuous *new*, won't the conditions necessary for its arising have to necessitate it at every point and moment, in every least fraction of objective time, without residue, until they will entirely constitute it? Where will its creativity, its not absolutely derived *power*, find refuge?

It will be well, in order to answer this objection, to recall and try to penetrate deeper into the nature of indeterminacy. One of the basic principles of indeterminacy — of *potentiality* in an active sense — is to be found in the fact of the *unity* of any psychic moment.

The unity–multiplicity of a psychic moment — an absolutely

[1] Cf. *A Philosophy of Potentiality*, pp. 9–10.

undivided, and multiple, *presence* — is not ultimately intelligible to us unless it is in the analogy of the *posse* (the verb, in the active sense), which is one and multiple at every moment — gradual, and inasmuch as it is so, multiple. Raymond Ruyer presents psychic unity as a "domaine absolu d'auto-survol." [2] This expression certainly reflects the truth, but it has only slight explicative value. The *unitas multiplex* is made more intelligible by the terms '*posse*,' '*Seinkönnen*,' [3] 'power' (intimate), and 'potentiality' (active). The terms 'synthesis' and 'dominion' presuppose the object as necessary to the being of the active subject and suggest preexistent or distinctly existent things and an initial duality between the undivided and the parts. Then I prefer the term 'can' or 'to have power' over 'to want,' because one's *will* more generally implies extrinsic purposiveness and comes close to a determinist scheme, where the end is given and the means are given, and the motives are equally given.

Let one use as many terms as one wishes to mean that several sensations (or perceptions, or representations, or other psychic facts) 'coalesce,' 'interpenetrate,' 'blend,' one shall always lapse into representations of barely concealed mechanism, representations that are provisional, irremediably exterior, suppositious, and, ultimately, obscure. If at any one of its moments the psyche is truly a unity and not an amalgam, that is so because of the possible infinite of every point and moment — because of an inherent potentiality that always and *ab initio* is an undecided moment and an inner infinite. A perception of red, for example, is identified with the memory of red, that is, of other sensations of red, and equally with the anticipation and in general with the image of red and of

---

[2] Raymond Ruyer, *Néo-finalisme* (Paris: Presses Universitaires de France, 1952), p. 110.

[3] Nicolaus Cusanus, *Vom Können-Sein, De possest* (Leipzig: F. Meiner, 1947), p. 35.

shades of such a color. But would this intimate identification be possible if any sensation of red weren't dynamically an infinite of itself? if at the root of all these representations there weren't a sole power, a more inexclusive potentiality capable of absorbing within itself as moments of itself every other potentiality beyond the limits of an ever-renewing objective existentiality? The potentiality–originality of one moment and that of another moment remain irremediably separate except for a unitary and more profound potentiality–originality, almost a *power* within a *power*, that *constitutes and includes* the one and the other moment.[4]

The positivity of the subjective being, furthermore, supposes an inner infinite because essentially it implies a possibility that is in some ways negative — in the very act in which it excludes it. 'Positivity' without an altogether inherent negative possibility would be inertia and would have no reality or psychic dimension.

Another reason for the intimate, ultimate unity of the psyche depends on the relationship, on the reciprocal immediate implication, of the motive values and modalities inherent in a true positivity — that is, in other terms, inherent in the creative ontological new (not a new of mere change, nor of a mere recombination of existent data).

Let us, in the first place, consider the relationship between the individual and the universal. There are those who seem to set individuality against universality as though they were incompatible realities and values, or as if they were devoid of any intimately genetic relation.[5] And yet it is clear that creativity itself, if it makes the

---

[4] Cf. my *Philosophy of Potentiality*, pp. 51–52.

[5] Cf. L. Brunschvigg, *L'expérience humaine et la causalité physique*: ". . . or, s'il y a une évidence dont il soit permis de parler en ce monde, n'est pas l'impossibilité que de l'individuel et du libre sortent l'universel et le nécessaire?" (Paris: F. Alcan, 1922), p. 36.

new, unicity, the incomparableness of several moments, and hence
individuality, into something intelligible, must identically contain
a value of universality — first of all because what is originally
active, what is in itself causal and final, is felt as infinitely possible
and as a value of universality (or of eternity), and as a likely universality of fact. To give an, I would almost say tangible, example,
these two moments of the spirit — the value of individuality and
the value of universality — are linked as two aspects of one same
reality (although in a prevalently visual representation) in the
following lines of Shakespeare:

> . . . When you speak, sweet,
> I'd have you do it ever. . . .
> When you do dance, I wish you
> A wave o' the sea, that you might ever do
> Nothing but that; move still, still so,
> And own no other function. Each your doing,
> So singular in each particular,
> Crowns what you are doing in the present deed,
> That all your acts are queens.
>
> *The Winter's Tale*, IV, 4, ll. 136–37, 140–46

But the sense of the infinite and the value of universality have
a deeper root in the extreme intrinsicality of the nature of positivity–
originality. The truths that seem to us to belong to the most intimate part of our being are generally felt as essential and, very
likely, as universal, exactly because they reflect a powerful intrinsic characterization of being in its originality in every one of its
moments. If, however, this powerful, ever-originary intrinsicality
of character links creatures in the sentiment of a common nature
or essence, then there is in other respects in this same intrinsicality
of character of the creative new, also the source of a stronger senti-

ment of reality of psychic activity — and the more so the more intensely creative it is. And this sense of intimate, underived, absolute, ultimate, genuine reality may equally be attributed to individuality, in one of its characteristic aspects, as a reality that is constitutive of its force: a reality immediately felt as truth, or with the strongest imprint of truth and of the absolute. The individual too depends on this twofold infinite — of potentiality and its absolutely intrinsic, underived characterization. Individuality lies not in the finite and the particular, rather it is in something that is *objectively* unattainable. Our profoundest identity is more intimate to us than any sense or figure of ourselves.

There are those who set the false dilemma: either necessity *or* contingency (or a *mixture* of necessity and contingency). Indeterminism convinces us, in an explicit thought, of what any one with a heart already knows: that principles are not laws or inert rules, but are of their own nature new in every one of their moments. The constancy of principles must not be interpreted as immobility and extratemporality, such as would cancel the essential new, for they are perennially being born from this ontological new, intrinsically characterized by its originality or creative newness, and they are, by virtue of their own nature, essentially new in every one of their moments. Thus our moral judgment must be literally *unprejudiced*, if it is going to have thoughtful reality and spiritual wholeness. Thus freedom bears essentially within itself the enormous weight— and the light — of its intrinsic nature, and not because it is conditioned. Thus charity — the universal ethic, not abstract or formal — is always new, and this character is essential to its value, as is admirably illustrated by the proposition: "He loves not at all who loves *enough*." [6]

[6] Paraphrase from Saint Francis of Sales, *Treatise on the Love of God*

The *finite* itself to a great extent has its value and its force —
negatively — from the inner infinite and from the *ab initio* unitive
nature of the *posse*. The finite, of course, as a reality divisible *ad
infinitum* and nevertheless ultimate reality, is an obscure, baffling
concept that leaves the mind in a quandary . . . In my judgment, as
I have said, the infinite (the inner, intensive, dynamic infinite) is
ultimately more intelligible than the finite.

In that which is *construction* there is (tendentially) *a retro*
causality, but in *creation* the active-subject is always the fleeting new
that, free from the shackles of the mechanical chain of cause and
effect, reveals its nature all the more. And it is particularly the poet
who recognizes in the originary new the node of values and the
aspects inherent in the positivity–originality of being in their germinally present relationships. I here quote some passages that in various ways refer to this 'essence':

> O known Unknown! . . .
> Such darling essence, . . .
>
> > Keats, *Endymion*, II, ll. 739–40

> Coming sometimes . . .
>   like a gentle whispering
> Of all the secrets of some wond'rous thing
> That breathes about us in the vacant air; . . .
>
> > Keats, *Sleep and Poetry*, ll. 27, 29–31

> Hear us, O satyr king!
>   . . .
> Dread opener of the mysterious doors
> Leading to universal knowledge . . .
>
> > Keats, *Endymion*, I, ll. 278, 288–89

(bk. 7, chap. 13), quoted in Arrigo Levasti, *I mistici* (Florence: Bemporad,
1926), 2:185.

> Wherein lies happiness? In that which becks
> Our ready minds to fellowship divine,
> A fellowship with essence; . . .
>
> Keats, *Endymion*, I, ll. 777–79

> Tutto ignori, e discerni
> Tutte le verita che l'ombra asconde.
>
> D'Annunzio, *Laudi*, III, *Il fanciullo*

Another fundamental motive-value that we can distinguish in this implication of values is the very eagerness for unity in the node of origin. But I won't dwell any longer on the relationships of principle or on the character of profound centrality of psychic reality, a centrality much more profound than any division or category, or 'complexes' or 'instincts' themselves. The above should suffice to make evident once more, should it ever be necessary, that physiological conditions cannot be the *constitutive* cause of a psychic moment — even of the most uncertain glimmer of sensitivity.

To a certain sensation, of the color red, for example, there correspond luminiferous radiations of a determined frequency and wave length. This does not mean, however, that red is a quantitative reality. This red — as sensation, as quality, as subjectivity — inasmuch as it *is*, will be a moment of unity, a moment of inner transparency or psychic amplitude, infinite identity–possibility of itself, a principle of active relation with other moments, and so forth. The luminiferous rays cease, the red ceases to be — except in the live imagination, conscious or subconscious; the rays return, the red comes back. The physiological and physical conditions decide the appearance and the continuous renewal of the red: but this is not why it is true that they constitute the simplest sensation of red in its originally active positivity. Sensation in its psychic reality can with verisimilitude always be imagined as an originally active principle, originally *one*, intrinsically final–causal — almost a spiritual pigment between the cause–conditions on the one hand, and, if they exist, the extrinsic ends in which it is immersed or in which it develops, on the other.

But if the last link in the causal neurophysiological chain cannot *constitute* the psychic moment, it can nevertheless provoke its rise and continuity — and this without depriving it of its jealous nature. I persist in holding that it isn't absurd or impossible for a qualitative force — without losing itself, without losing the undivided and the infinite of the power to be and a fundamentally constitutive, not merely factual, nonmeasurability — to present a unitary resistance to a reality that is in a sense divisible, materially extended, derivative, inert.[7]

What can one say of the psychological antecedents? Will these be able intimately and rigorously to necessitate the new moment?

Life is all a struggle against the fugacity of time and a struggle to constitute itself in durable forms, but its reality is in the present moment, in the throb of the fleeting new. The constant and universal phenomenon of reproductivity in living nature and conservation itself — if *conservation* does not mean mere passivity, inertia — perhaps reflect a principle of transcendence of the actual, an obstinate and vigilant force, that could still be interpreted as belonging to the profound intrinsicality of nature of the very positivity–originality of the subjective being. But how can the present moment promote the next new moment without completely stripping it of its originality? And, most importantly, how can it identify itself in the new moment and give it its own stamp, if that doesn't yet exist and *is not*? And still positivity–creativity itself — active potentiality itself — seems essentially to tend toward the future. "Through the

---

[7] Cf. chapter 3 of this volume.

darkness and the splendour of the centuries, loud or dumb,/Shines and wanes and shines the spirit, *lit with love of life to come*," Swinburne says.[8] Be that as it may, the new (creative, ontological) in order to be new must ever perish. And, no less obviously, total derivation excludes it.

There may be, between one moment and another, a relation of intimate causality, and this by way of an essential identification through a common nature, through the multiple intrinsic characterization of psychic activity itself in its perennial originality. Precisely how this identification *ex intrinseco* takes place is not as clear as perhaps we should like it to be: but we are certainly dealing with something more convincing than any process coming about through association, as it is generally conceived.

We must keep well in mind that whatever is creative would cease to be so if it were transmitted. The conditions of a quality can be hereditary or transmissible, but quality has its own actual origin for which there absolutely cannot be a substitute. Philosophers and psychologists who acknowledge a creative element in psychic reality nevertheless pass over this difficulty, and it seems to me that they talk of creativity lightly, thus implying that it is transmitted or preserved. Bergson himself often says that the psychic past "prolongs itself," "preserves itself," "continues," endures in the present.[9] These expressions, literally interpreted, make us risk falling back into the scheme of extrinsic causal concatenation, through which there is nothing but derivation. Yet life comes from the new, not from the old. We may delude ourselves into thinking

[8] Algernon Charles Swinburne, *The Altar of Righteousness*, 1, v. 3; the italics are mine.

[9] Cf., e.g., *Durée et simultanéité, à propos de la théorie d'Einstein* (Paris: F. Alcan, 1922), p. 55.

that we can derive everything from antecedents, from instincts, from cause-conditions, but the most intimate, the purest value has a deeper and *truer* origin; and perhaps it is recognizable by the imprint of a greater impersonality and innocence. Everything that is profoundly real is creative. Life creates and recreates itself continuously in successive processes and developments, in contact with matter and with its own forms: continuously it lights itself, specifies, enriches itself; ever new, renewing the past in itself. The new *renews* in itself the past, which is altogether different from being produced by the past; the new continues the past, actively, which is altogether different from being its (inert) continuation. The present invests and draws the past along with it by virtue of a *new* creator that knows in itself its rich germ. One inherits the conditions favorable or necessary to (not necessarily sufficient for) life, but not properly life, which is always a gift *a fronte*. Even in a mathematical equation, for example $2+2=4$, the first moment conditions, but does not generate, the second: for there to be the second moment there needs *newly* to be the idea of the finite, with all that it immediately implies; or otherwise there shall be no thought, no psychic reality, but only automatism.

But, finally, can the present moment provoke through intimate causality — that is, through an identification in the intrinsic nature of the '*new*' — the next moment, *which yet is not*? Certainly not. We can nevertheless avoid this difficulty by supposing in the subconscious, or in the unknown, a continuous creativity — however germinal and elementary. For in the hypothesis of a perennially creative new, the problem of its arising at a given time rather than at another does not present itself, and the actual moment could always find the *new* in which to identify itself *ex intrinseco*, in which to lose itself and light itself anew in the full originality of the spirit and the supreme reality of the present. And this latent, but nonetheless real, continuity would be the basis of any solicitation of the new for essential identification in the next moment, and of the continuity of conscious life in the incessant, and in a certain measure ever-independent, origin of a true positivity.

Another difficulty I would like to dwell upon is the following: once one admits that force is coessential and coextensive with thought and psychic reality in general,[10] then one shall also have to hold that creation of thought is creation of force, and particularly that indeterminacy implies creation of force, indeed *self-creation* of force — something that for many may seem heresy. I mean to say an originary force, not merely functional or derivative. And I mean psychic, active, creative indeterminacy: leaving aside *chance*, relative or absolute, which is neither creativity nor value, and which does not concern psychic indeterminacy, except where the unforeseen in chance may favor creative spontaneity in the development of thought.

Movement as causal and final or purposive in itself, as *causa sui*, absolutely cannot be understood. And, too, the creation of intimate force and therefore of movement, for instance in someone who tries to move a heavy object, may not seem very plausible. But the creation of force, in an effort, will be better understood if we turn our thoughts to effort as a force of concentration. A moment of concentration is an essentially qualitative reality. It represents for us the one-in-the-many, a qualitative multiplicity, a *presence*, the actual infinite of potentiality or indeterminacy, an *intensity* — which is a subjective and qualitative term. The whole of one's soul, the *live* part of being or of thought, and, for instance, the desperation in not being able to save oneself or others, are or can be involved in a moment of effort; nor can one tell apart in such a moment what is

[10] Cf. chapter 3 of this volume.

force of concentration from the whole of psychic reality, in that moment or in that individual. The creative quintessence, the undivided, shines through everywhere in a force that is not merely functional or one of relation. The mechanist psychologist will object that the perception of effort resolves itself in muscular and other sensations. We concede this: nevertheless in those muscular sensations we still find the spirit. The mechanist will above all object that, as a matter of fact, in each determined case the expended calories are the equivalent of those introduced with the ingested food; but I think this has not been demonstrated sufficiently.[11]

Lived force is intimately known as *having power* (in the active sense), in the first place for the production, and we can also say for the creation, of movement and for outward action. Force as a condition of relations in physics (and in this acceptation it is certainly right to give up the term 'force') cannot make us reject as a residue of animistic principles the true force, something truly active, always originally new — that which is always implicit or explicit in our ordinary conversation, and in the thought, in the myths, and in the religions of all times.

It will be objected that when we speak, for example, of force of spirit, of the force of passion, of affections, of sentiment, of the force of sacrifice, of love, of hate, of the force of attention, of the force of persuasion, or again of the force of concentration, or of building up force, and so forth, we consider unspecified appearances as ultimate reality and we return to discredited conceptions. Truly, it seems to me that we are meeting naked reality, and that he who obstinately perceives as unreal, irrational, and incomprehensible what is not subject to being measured is in the wrong. For we can also look for this nonderivative intimate force in its many aspects,

---

[11] Cf. my *Philosophy of Potentiality*, p. 25.

which imply and confirm one another. This intimate force will be lacking in quantitative determinacy and in objectively given existentiality: but it is indeed this radical indeterminacy that lets us conceive it all the more as an active indeterminacy and as a real force — not merely derivative, functional, or relation, and in itself inert.

Another difficulty has, we shall say, a cosmological character. We ask ourselves: How did life begin? We know that no germ of life can hitherto have crossed interstellar or interplanetary space. Further, we know that in all probability the earth has had a limited period of existence, all the more so as a habitable planet. Now we can make various hypotheses: (1) Being, as an ever-originary urge and an intrinsic causality–finality, must, we may think, have always been — a perennial incipience that has never had a beginning. The hypothesis therefore suggests itself that life originates everywhere and always, wherever there are favorable conditions, or wherever decidedly unfavorable conditions do not exclude it. (2) Life can traverse space in forms and ways altogether unknown to us. (3) Life derives from matter. (4) It does not derive from matter, but the principle of subjectivity is already — either wholly or in part — *constitutive* of matter, that is, of the matter–energy of microscopic physics (according to what has been variously and authoritatively suggested).

If we put aside the first two hypotheses, this dilemma then presents itself: either life on earth derives from matter — something that I think should be excluded — or we have to admit that while it does not derive from matter, its principle is constitutive of matter itself; that is, is already present and active (something analogous to the *posse*) in the nuclear physics of the earth or of any celestial body. Indeterminacy — the concept of creativity — leads in this way to a conception that is ultimately monist (in the psychic sense).

By way of conclusion, and referring as well to my previous works, I shall say that in my judgment, indeterminacy is contradicted neither by facts nor by logic.[12] There remains, against indeterminacy, a metaphysical judgment. We may ask ourselves the *why* of being as an intrinsic causality–finality (finality in the sense of inner purposiveness), or as an ever-originary urge. Materialistic determinism largely eliminates such orders of problems as those concerning the *why* of being and of the universe: in fact the existence *ab aeterno* of blind energies, *a tergo*, is more easily accepted as a final datum, one needing no explanation. Indeterminacy — the concept of creativity — makes our world intelligible according to the profound logic of the *logos*, but it unlocks dizzying problems, for in certain respects inertia seems more easily understood than, ultimately, something truly active.

[12] See particularly my *Il concetto dell'indeterminazione*, chaps. 2 and 3.

CHAPTER 5

The Subjective Infinite and the Undivided

The inner infinite and the undivided have the common foundation of an ultimate reality. I do not intend to deal with the objective infinite — the infinitely great and the infinitely small; or the infinitely removed in space or time; or the mathematical infinite; or the theological infinite conceived as the opposite of all that is *finite*, of all that is earthly. Although, indeed, even the objective infinite draws its intuitive value partly from the inner infinite in its subjective, originally active, intensive, intrinsically final value.

The terms 'indeterminate' and 'indefinite' are obviously inadequate to signify precisely this inner infinite, which is an infinite of actuality and tension, implying the sense of something that is never completed and a finality that is absolutely intrinsic to the nature of being — *being* as activity, as an ever-original craving.

One might interpret the word 'infinite' etymologically, in a negative sense, as the negation of 'finite,' the *finite* being conceived as reality *par excellence*. But basically the term 'infinite' has a positive meaning (and the 'finite' acquires significance from it). For the inner infinite is the sense and reality of (active) potentiality; it is the immediate value of a *possibility* that is actually experienced; it makes the force and reality of the act itself.

The idea of a beyond-the-limit is instantly implied in the representation of a limit, and it may simply indicate a factual reality in accordance with objective abstract thought. Nevertheless, the idea of something beyond all limits, beyond all reality and comparison, does express an absolute value; and such a value properly belongs to the active infinite in its underived originality.

But this potentiality–infinity, which is above all realized in intensity, albeit within a limited compass, must be sought not only, for instance, in the infinite of liberty, grief, or anguish, or pain, or desire, but equally so and on all occasions in the *living* moment of creativity and even in the least sign of a psychic presence.

What is the common root of the subjective infinite and the undivided?

No less than the subjective infinite, the undivided must be conceived, it seems, as an essentially active, creative reality — a power understood not to fall into the *given*, the *finite*, the *divided*, the *inert*.

The subjective infinite (internal, intensive, purposeful; originally and creatively dynamic) has an undivided character. If, for example, I try with all my strength to pull the handle of a dynamometer, I feel that my effort is one and undivided. If it were divided, my effort would be reduced to a series of finite and fixed elements belonging to the world of objectively determined existents, deprived of potentiality, whether they were in motion or not; and this would exclude the dynamic infinite of indeterminacy as a subjective value and reality.

The undivided implies multiplicity, though the multiplicity is in a sense annulled; otherwise its meaning would be incomprehensible. The multiplicity of the act (assuming that we do not have here mere mechanical necessity) is in the first place postulated by a negative possibility whereby liberty–necessity differs from literal,

mechanical, inert necessity. This element of the *possible* is absolutely intrinsic in the act, is indeed its very force and substance. The
principle of indivisibility of the infinite may be understood if by
'infinite' we mean 'Absolute,' as an attribute of God: in this case
the undivided finds its justification in a sort of omnipotence that
comprehends and constitutes the whole. But obviously I am not
dealing here with a transcendent power; what I mean is the *possible*
as a reality that is absolutely native to the actuality of the most vivid
present. The intensive infinite that inheres in the possibility of being
is undivided: it is undivided as value, as force, as real and genuine
positivity. We are returning here to the concept of *posse* as an ultimate foundation of both the undivided and the subjective infinite.

Love is jealous of its infinity, just as it is jealous of its *oneness*;
and this is so because, in the first place, this oneness — originality,
inimitability — has its only possibility in the intensive infinite of
(psychic) indeterminacy.

The foundation of both the undivided and the subjective infinite
seems to consist in an element that is creatively active, in potentiality
as actual reality.

Active potentiality is also — and it is so essentially — a craving
for realization and form. But before I deal at length with this and
other implications of this concept of potentiality–creativity, let me
point out certain deficiencies of an aesthetic theory that seems to
lack just such a concept — the concept of a reality that is not merely
derivative.

In a book that has been well received, Susanne K. Langer asserts
that the work of art is 'illusion,' 'semblance,' 'appearance,' 'symbol,'
'abstraction.' [1] The terms 'symbol' and 'abstraction' are commonly

[1] *Feeling and Form* (London: Routledge & Kegan Paul, 1959). Cf.

used in reference to certain forms of art. But a work of art is essentially something quite different from a symbol, if by symbol we mean, according to common usage, what stands for something else. As to the term 'abstraction,' it reflects a very poor philosophy whereby what is 'concrete' and opposed to abstract is anything that is material and external. Such a view ignores true concreteness — the integrity, wholeness, non-onesidedness of spirit in its expressive spontaneity.

The term 'symbol' can have various meanings. The 'symbol' can be conventionally understood as an unmistakable and irreplaceable expression of something that is other than itself. Or it can express the sense of the vivid presence, in the symbol itself, of the thing or idea that is supposed to be symbolized. So we might say of a woman that she "symbolizes grace" to indicate precisely that she is a singular example *and a reality* of this quality or value.

In physics, mathematical symbols replace more and more the concepts and phenomena themselves — handy symbols that are easily abstracted from any ontological reference, although some such reference, I think, is never entirely lost and may be an incentive to research. But it is all too obvious that a work of art cannot be reduced to something of merely instrumental value; in art we want to touch an ultimate, actual, subjective origin.

The term 'symbol' is also used in reference to artistic activity in order to explain how repressed and openly inadmissible things may find, as it were, an outlet and be expressed surreptitiously in a work of art. The symbol through which these repressed desires are expressed could, however, be a mere scrawl and give no impression of artistic achievement; nor is it at all clear that the essence of art

Philosophy in a New Key: A Study in the Symbolism of Reason, Rite, and Art (Cambridge: Harvard University Press, 1942).

proceeds from a symbolic character of this kind. Nevertheless, if this mode of indirect expression were a general occurrence, the term 'symbol' might be appropriate here, even if it did not fundamentally concern the value of a work of art.

The actual ontological (subjective) reality of any aspect is already an immense reality — not because of what it symbolizes, but because of what it *is*. A symbolic character is often attributed to expression because of its supposed relation to a vaster, cosmic reality; but this relation is one thing, and the intimate implications of art — which are its very being, its expression — are something else. The reality that the artist expresses resides in the very act of expressing it. Any theory or conception that tends to separate form and content, representation and the thing represented, symbol and the thing symbolized, turns us away from art.

Form — in art as well as, perhaps, in all of living nature — is, in short, not an instrumental value: it is a value intrinsically final or purposive, in itself causal. A work of art does not turn or depend on anything else for its reality, because, I repeat, it is an immediate actualization and revelation of an inextricable nucleus of values absolutely inherent in a present origin or in an intimate activity or in form (understood as a formative principle): it is form in its value of creativity, of oneness, in its value of infinite transparency in itself and by itself (potentiality) as well as in the strength of the powerful characterization intrinsic to its originality (value of universality) . . . And reducing art to a symbol, something unreal replacing something else (be it a thing or a concept), is tantamount to denying the value of art itself.

But the theoretical construction according to which a work of art is an illusion, a symbol (in itself unreal), an abstraction (equally in itself unreal) of another reality, has its basis in a manner of thinking that is dogmatically mechanistic, for this is how Susanne Langer expresses herself: "All forces that cannot be scientifically established and measured must be regarded, from a philosophical standpoint, as illusory; if, therefore, such forces seem to be a part of our direct experience, they are 'virtual,' i.e., non-actual semblances." [2] 'Non-actual' means here 'unreal,' without reservation.

Indeterminacy — that is, potentiality as an actual value and reality — is essentially averse to being measured. I do not mean here the 'essential indeterminacy' of subatomic physics, which concerns only the technical impossibility of measuring a phenomenon due to the interference of the means whereby it is measured, and so on indefinitely with all the other means with which one might want to measure the means that interfered with the measuring in the first place; such indeterminacy does not necessarily have any ontological significance, whether objective or subjective. In an ontological sense, and with a view to an ultimate reality, scientists sometimes refer to chance; but relative chance leads us back to numberless causes, and absolute chance cannot be proved since we cannot prove that causes don't exist that are unknown to us, minimal though they may be. The 'essential indeterminacy' of physics shows that determinism in physics *is not* proved, but it does not prove indeterminism.

Psychic indeterminacy consists in an intensive infinite for which it is absolutely vital that it be undivided and not measurable. This intensive infinite cannot be reducible to a measurable existential objectivity, to a series of existing data, without being lost completely. The possible has value and force just because and insofar as it is experienced as such. This core of subjective being will never be reached except by *ex novo* identification with another possible that has been experienced, and that will always be a nonmeasurable unity–infinity.

[2] *Feeling and Form*, p. 188.

In a world consisting of objectively determined existents and extrinsic relations between given elements, there is no room for any creativity. Langer constantly uses such terms as 'creative,' 'creativity,' 'creation,' 'create'; but sometimes it looks as if 'creative' means something quite fictitious and illusory compared with natural reality. It is a fact that she often uses these terms but never stops to clarify their meaning (which is admittedly not her fault alone). She informs us only that she uses the word 'creation' "in full awareness of its problematic character." [3]

Art transforms everything into the undivided-infinite of quality. Indeed, this transformation may also be found in language generally, but it is especially characteristic of art. There is here a difference of degree, not of nature. Art is always a discovery of actual cause, that is, of a present origin, in a manner that is more or less implicit, or even explicit.[4] This is equally a motive-value of philosophy, but philosophy subordinates the immediacy of this discovery, and therefore its processes have a systematic character; they are, in a certain sense, utilitarian (instrumental), to the detriment of truth's sources.

The past gives nothing but extrinsic causality; every intimate development must take place *ex novo*: it can only be conceived as a perpetual absorption and renewal in an activity originally active. We do not express ourselves well, or we do so only approximately, if we say that thought 'opens,' 'expands,' 'projects itself,' 'overflows,' 'widens.' Of the past only cause-conditions remain, an inert and blind reality; only the actuality of thought contains in its essential novelty the fertile seed whereby it absorbs the past *ad infinitum*,

[3] Ibid., p. 40.
[4] Cf. my *Il concetto dell'indeterminazione*, part 2, chap. 5.

in an ever-renewed rose of values. If this *activity* were literally maintained as it is, transmitted or inherited, it would ultimately be nothing but inertia: it must of necessity be always new. The ultimate process of becoming can only be resolved as an ever-original activity — however conditioned it may be. Now art is indeed, I would almost say, a vindication, and a revelation, a presence of this actuality that is ever final and causal.

The absolute can only be sought in a principle that is originally active, unless we indulge in the hopeless task of referring perpetually to something else. We are all immersed in the absolute; but it is the artist who has a clearer, more intimately and profoundly cognitive consciousness of this reality that is not merely derivative. He is less subordinate to extrinsic purposes. He craves for an ultimate reality that is not composite and not to be decomposed — not consisting in mere relation; for an origin that belongs only to itself; for a force that yearns to be in the very act of being; for a value that is not entirely secondary, or instrumental, or conventional; for a reality powerfully characterized by the impact of the originality–causality that is absolutely intrinsic to it, and therefore felt as a value of intimate truth, universality, and eternity, so that the feeling for it is as strong as the originality of the act is real and pure, as strong as its quality of uniqueness and inimitability.

There can be no theory of art without the notion of an actual origin.

According to Langer, the work of art not only lacks substance, but also (and this is a common opinion) has no intrinsic value of a cognitive-philosophical order.[5] It would be interesting to know what kind of cognitive value is at issue. But if the subtle spark of cognition were not in it, the much-celebrated value of art would be an imposture.

[5] Cf. *Feeling and Form*, p. 396.

Potentiality as understood here is already a *form*, because it is a psychic presence, an original intimate value of the infinite; it is a form, above all, because it is essentially an urge or exigency for actualization. Doubtlessly potentiality itself tends to transcend all forms in an infinite transparency, and it is felt as such; and there is a fertile, inexhaustible conflict between potentiality on the one hand and the limit on the other, or the data that, in a certain respect, are inherent to form itself in whatever sense it may have. But potentiality is the very heart of creativity, and creativity is a formative principle (active, constitutive), an immediate plasticity. In brief, we shall say that form is an essential motive-value in the nucleus of values that are inherent in the ontological new (subjectively understood).

But the ontology of form requires a careful examination in which we are forced to make hypotheses and conjectures. Once we admit that thought is not absolutely and literally identical with its physiological conditions, we must suppose that in order to interact with these it must possess a force of its own. This X force will not be the energy of physical matter — or we would once again be faced with the problem of the effective interrelation between the psychic and this force. It will not be the physical matter–energy made up of molecules, atoms, protons, mesons, neutrons, photons, dynamic units, electromagnetic radiations, and so forth, in reference to which it would also be difficult to conceive how, at every fleeting thought, it can arise and dissolve. This X force will have to participate in the creativity of thought — it will have to *be* thought. (By 'thought' I mean, through antonomasia, psychic reality in general.)

This power — or force — will have to be all one with thought, with its inner transparency, with its intensity, for which it is absolutely vital that it be undivided, immeasurable, irreducible to determined existents; it will be all one with the value of thought, its reality of potentiality, of intimate and immediate causality–finality, all one with every deepest intrinsic characterization of the subjective being.

We are therefore obliged to entertain the hypothesis that a force or power essentially qualitative has the capability of intensifying its resistance, of concentrating, solidifying in some way, and dissolving, *at every instant*, and of exerting a direct action on the physical — or of being subjected to it — without, however, sharing its nature. And certainly it is an arduous task to conceive how a force–intelligence that is not measurable should, without losing itself, come into contact with a mass of reality that is extensive and virtually measurable. And this in the very moment of its greatest luminosity and effectiveness, in the moment of expression and realization.

Furthermore, this power that participates in the creativity of thought, and that *is* thought, should produce physical energy, a quantity of movement; and this in contradiction to the physical law of the conservation of energy.[6]

It is also worthwhile remembering that so-called 'objectified thought' ('fossilized,' 'petrified,' 'thought out' . . .) cannot serve as a bridge between thought and matter. Though it has aspects that are analogous to those of our scheme concerning matter, it is not physical matter–energy, but reality of thought; and it is always, in every detail, in every numerical unit, an infinite, possible identity of itself with itself, felt and experienced as such — and not a formal identity in an abstract and absolute sense. It is always an actual reality of thought, though extremely one-sided. In the psychic dimension each element is an infinite possibility of itself — an in-

[6] Concerning these difficulties, cf. my *Philosophy of Potentiality*, chap. 2, "The Immediate Existentiality of Thought," and see chapter 3 of this volume.

finite absence as well as an infinite presence.

On the other hand, the yearning of thought to realize itself in matter — to transform matter as a condition into matter as a sensible object — could not be explained if an effective interrelation were not possible. In fact, this interrelation between the physical and the psychic is made every day more evident and it cannot be denied in good faith. It would certainly be futile, moreover, to seek refuge in the idea of a pre-established harmony between the physical and the psychic — or to deny either one. The more so since even if subatomic physics showed us that there is in the energy of matter a subjective principle, an inner element, an intrinsic immediate purposiveness, an activity–creativity or noninertia, we would still have the problem of the relation between psychic reality and the physical reality of our ordinary experience.

Undoubtedly the interrelation exists. But why is it absurd to think of a resistance that does not belong to physical reality and yet is capable of working upon the physical? Why is it absurd to think that the psyche can create for itself a near-materiality, without losing in it its active potentiality and its indivisibility? We are faced with something perhaps incomprehensible, but not absurd.

Our first intuition of a clash is that of some force within us able to resist even if it is not properly matter. When struggling, we feel our force as indeterminate in the extreme, free, all our own: the extrinsic causal effect does not really belong to it — does not belong to us. If I apply my strength against an object, the undivided quality of my strength comes from my inmost depth, from an actual potentiality; it is a total psychic reality, and as long as my force is alive and effective the material contact does not seem to impinge at all upon its nature.

It is not enough to assert that the intuition of a nonphysical originally active force — a force, therefore, that is not merely functional, simply relative, derivative, inertial, such that indeed could hardly be called a force at all — means falling back into conceptions that are outmoded, mystical, anthropomorphic, animistic, etc. The idea of a nonphysical force is far from being absurd — once we agree that thought is not a purely physical reality.

In conclusion we must, I think, recognize a formative power that is thought itself, but considered particularly in its character of externality through which it can work effectively upon the physiological processes.

I call *primary plasma* this hypothetical X reality that is at one and the same time thought (interiority, psychic presence) and capacity for external relations. We might imagine that in germinal forms, the natural incompatibility between the primary plasma and the physiological and physical conditions might be more easily overcome; then the original plasma itself and the physiological conditions would become somehow congenial with one another.

This immediate, active, creative plastic reality will have to be present, in varying measure and degree, in every intuition, whether expressed or not. But we might perhaps detect its work more directly in the simplicity and spiritual wholeness of the works that belong to the golden centuries of art; and always, wherever the element *creation* prevails over the element *construction*.

The very word 'origin,' unless we wish to pass over its obvious meaning, implies *something from nothing*. And the idea of a perpetual and, ultimately, independent origin is no less perturbing than that of a merely derivative world.

The positivity of being is a fact of the utmost importance that perhaps nobody would be willing to admit if it were not that we can conceive it in the analogy of an intimate experience that has a thousand names and aspects.

Such a positivity implies a negative possibility — without which it would cease to be *positivity*. It would be the mere emergence of something, chance, derivation, inertia. *Activity* differs from inertia just because it contains a negative possibility — a negativity that may be continually held in check, neutralized, but is all one with the very concept of positivity. Indeed, this *uncertainty*, always overcome and yet never completely overcome (except after the accomplishment of an act, when the act is no longer, in itself, a reality of thought or spirit), this *nonmechanical certainty* is essential to any intrinsic and non-idle purposiveness, to potentiality itself and to the inner infinite; it seems to contain the secret and perhaps the ultimate explanation of the psychic dimension, of the psychic *presence*. Because of the negative possibility that is its intimate implication, this positivity of which I speak must be defined as *possibility*. Naturally I do not intend an abstractly conceived possibility among alternatives, each one of which would exclude it. This *possibility* is the soul of the act! Possibility (in an active sense), intensive infinite, and creativity are, we can maintain, one sole reality.[7]

The idea implied in something originally new that is not mere change, the idea of an activity that is value and not chance, and that is not literal necessity or constriction, is reflected to some extent in many words of our language, as, for instance, 'liberty, 'responsibility,' 'will,' 'volition,' 'power,' 'hope,' 'faith,' 'love,' 'hatred,' 'activity,' and so on. But these terms do not seem to be explicit and definitive enough if they have to mean that which is originally new, new in its ultimate and most intimate nature.

The terms 'origin,' 'source,' 'genesis,' and others do not exclude

---

[7] In this frame of reference we should set positivity side by side with faith, which is essentially creative. Faith somehow includes the possibility of an intimate doubt without which it could not exist actively and would not really be *faith* at all; see Nicola Abbagnano, *Filosofia religione scienza*, 2d ed. (Turin: Taylor, 1960), pp. 61 ff.

the simple emergence of something, which might also be interpreted in a mechanistic sense.

The term 'autogenesis,' and also 'self-made,' 'self-realizing,' 'self-originating,' and others formed in the same way are not really adequate because they posit the *self* as an object. This might lead to the false assumption of a fixed existent, which would be made to create something through a merely functional process of extrinsic causality, *a retro*. The formative principle should be inherent in what is being formed. Creative potentiality does not really belong to a preexisting subject, but always to the *new*, as an active subject that absorbs the past in itself. Creativity is identical with actual being or it will never exist.

Thus also the word 'creation' could be misunderstood as creation of something *ab extrinseco*, which would not be properly creation, but a process of mere construction and reconstruction by means of given elements — and creation only insofar as it is permeated with genuine activity and original invention; insofar, that is, as it is not strictly a mere construction in an abstract sense.

More adequate, therefore, seem the expressions that do not point to a distinct object, as precisely 'creativity,' 'activity,' 'activation,' 'potency' (an intimate power, as a verb, in an active sense), 'potentiality,' 'intrinsic finality or purposiveness,' 'exigency' (an ever-original exigency), 'positivity,' 'originality.'

The distinction between subject and object, posited as a necessary condition of psychic reality, seems to me one of the most dismal errors in the whole history of philosophy. There is the object as an inferential datum, especially in the knowledge of physical reality. But essentially the subject is already in itself substance, an intimate light and value; and there is no reason to conceive it as something that has to reflect upon itself in order to be, as though it were nothing in itself alone. Any representation, or perception, even the so-called objectified thought, insofar as it is a reality of thought, insofar as it is quality, can be nothing else but activity, active subject. As long as the so-called object is a psychic reality, it is always activity, and there is always a principle of mutual identification *ad infinitum* between any representation and the so-called 'I.' Qualities live by their own life. Conscience is originally and inextricably an intimate value and plasticity; nor is it comprehensible why and how it should arise from the position of the object. What is intimately known is only known as an active quality with which we are identified, that is, it is only known as an active subject.

Or shall we give to the term 'object' a purposive sense? According to the most common way of thinking, purposiveness or finality is understood as extrinsic purposiveness, which implies an instrumental and utilitarian point of view, a fixed goal that is itself inert. We forget a reality of activity whose purpose is cause and substance. That is, we forget a purposiveness that is absolutely intrinsic to activity itself, where activity–purposiveness does not primarily, essentially, depend upon a distinct subject, since it is just this purposiveness that is the subject and agent. And especially in art not only the intrinsic idea but also the means become subject–agents, active qualities, indistinguishable from the thought of the artist.

Naturally I do not wish to deny that the distinction between subject and object ('object' also understood as a term of thought) may be justified in certain respects — as, for instance, when we wish to stress a psychic distance, as it were, between the strictly intentional element of the subject, on the one hand, and the representations themselves, whether they be considered in their relative inertia or in their powerful, vast, independent intrinsicality of origin on the other. But to see in the position of the object the condition for the emergence of conscience seems to me to ignore the primary reality of conscience itself and make it dependent upon causes that are profoundly inadequate. For conscience is subjective *being*, or a form or moment of being, and participates in its radical nature; it is indeed its first and most open witness.

The term 'to be' is used in many ways, but it has one meaning that is particularly unambiguous, profound, and rich: subjective being as *substance*, as self-sustained reality, uncompounded, un-decomposable, underived, profoundly characterized by the very fact of being; as an inimitable and irreplaceable reality; as an ever-original yearning, as an originally active activity, as creativity, and therefore as something unique and new; as an ever-original force, plasticity, or form; as a *presence* or an inner transparency — the undivided infinite of the value, and reality, of potentiality actually experienced as such; as an absolutely intrinsic purposiveness; as an inexhaustible mutual implication of this and other fundamental values as well as the spontaneous and vital integration of their unity; as an *intrinsic* characterization of being itself in these aspects: an absolute intrinsicality of characterization that imprints the very novelty and uniqueness of single forms — and is sometimes known, not as an eternity of fact, but, in a certain sense, as a value of eternity.

Among these primary aspects the one richest in problems is that of an absolute intrinsicality of character of the actual origin insofar as it is really *origin*. For it is difficult to resist the temptation to set up as a static, unchangeable, extratemporal entity (or law, or idea) the constancy — or essential identity or principle — of this ever-original positivity of being. On the other hand, such identity–eternity, far from giving the desired explanation of value and of the psyche, would be their absolute negation; in any case it would be something of quite a different nature from these. And even if we supposed an all-comprehensive power, active in all kinds of activity–originality, the problem would shift to the nature of this power: its constant identity could only depend upon an intrinsic characteriza-tion ever renewed.

The identity of my own self in this present moment with my same self of a moment ago is certainly favored and assured by the permanence of physiological cause-conditions, but the substance of this identification always lies in the constant intrinsic characterization of the new insofar as it is new. This natural intrinsic character of *active* being contains the secret of any unity and continuity of the single individual and of all understanding and communion among living creatures. In objective existentiality, in the scheme of objectively determined entities, deprived of potentiality, deprived of intimate actuality or real activity or the ever-renewed quality of intrinsic characterization, there can only be external relations, relations of a mutual conditionality; there are no immediate intimate kinships and harmonies, and all true unity is a problem far from being solved. The nucleus of values implied in the ontological new or in the original new cannot form itself in absolute unity unless it arises originally: according to its nature it needs the annihilation of every form insofar as it is formed and divisible — or the perfect oblivion of all form.

A living being is profoundly stirred when it perceives a principle or an essence that it has in common with other living beings — in compassion, in love, in intimate truth. Now will this common essence — or 'intrinsic infinite,' as I call it — have no reality except in the act?

This supreme novelty–intrinsicality of characterization I am dwelling upon will hide itself in the least perception — and in the little seed of a flower. In the concurrence of cause-conditions it will make its nature always more evident, always renewing and recovering itself. And will it always be essentially new; will it have no reality except in the fleeting act?

I am convinced that nothing can reconcile the intimate creativity of value with its constant nature, unless it be an absolutely intrinsic characterization inherent to creativity itself. The intrinsic characterization of subjective being exists only in the single realization, in the process of actualization; it depends upon it intelligibly and absolutely. The very concept of universality must be traced back to that of a powerful intimate characterization that is absolutely — and intelligibly — intrinsic to the novelty–creativity of the single act. Unfortunately, it is true that the intrinsicality–eternity of the creative act can also feed the clumsy pride of the super-man; but in its more intimate and profound judgments it is and will be an appeal for less exclusiveness, less misunderstanding, less cruelty.

The value of eternity inherent in an actual origin does not at all imply a factual eternity — neither a static, enduring eternity nor an extratemporal reality. Actual origin implicitly contains the idea of an infinitely possible actualization — but such as that which expresses the very force of a *causa sui*, the core or pulse of what has in itself its own cause: not through reference to a factual eternity, of which we have no guarantee and no certainty, or to an eternity of a kind that might be considered negligible in itself, like the eternal preservation of a clod of earth. If an intimate value touches us more closely than a utilitarian or pragmatic or conventional value, and more than the law of the state, it is due to the profound nature of being in its originality–necessity.

Perhaps it is particularly in music that the infinite of a potentiality that is actually experienced and almost tangible reveals itself, and along with it the reality of an infinite equally experienced but more profound: the infinite of intrinsic characterization, powerfully and absolutely intrinsic, inherent to potentiality itself. And I must also say that the one and the other potentiality cannot easily be distinguished, for the former bears in itself, now more, now less, the value and the force — and the mystery — of its powerful intrinsicality of nature, and, that is to say, of its truth.

The inspired creative act must abandon itself to this virgin, infinite intrinsicality of origin — an *undivided* that is even more profound. The simplicity of art depends upon a continuous recovery of the *undivided*, which belongs to creative potentiality and its two-fold infinite.

Some proclaim the nonintelligibility of life, starting as they do from a mechanical or almost mechanical point of view, and they take pleasure in denying the reality of thought. According to the conception I have set forth here, what is most alive is most intelligible. The more alive and the purer the originality of thought, the more luminous, irresistible, and subtle are the kinships of original values that arise therefrom. The more a thought is creative in its deepest sense, the more it is felt as intimately true and as a value of universality. For ideas have a value of universality in inverse proportion to their abstraction.

CHAPTER 6

Art and the Ontological New

Each psychical moment, given that it is not totally derived — and excluding the hypothesis of absolute chance — contains by definition an element of actual positivity, of noninertia.

I use the terms 'creativity' and 'creation' to mean the same thing; but I often prefer using the term 'creativity,' because 'creation' suggests something that preexists and creates, while the principle of creation can only be absolutely present, intrinsic in the act, constitutive of the act.

The concept of creation is variously defined, especially in regard to art. Creation, as I hold, is the actualization of a node of values implicit in an intimate, active power-to-be. But since, according to this definition, creation (or creativity) is one with and the same thing as *activity*, insofar as activity is really *active*, that is, not wholly derived and not fortuitous, the term itself, simply identified with the quick of activity, loses in this acceptation its specific meaning. Indeed, in order for 'creation' to be eminently present — and in conformity with the prevailing usage of the word — the potentiality–positivity of the subjective being (that is, being as active subject, as principle of activity), or this node of values, must reach a high degree of intensity — and this in a gradation without apparent break. The spiritual concreteness of the creative new (the ontological new, the new of reality, not a mere change of previously existing elements) must prevail fundamentally over mechanism, habit, causality–conditionality, extrinsic construction based on given elements, abstract will, arbitrariness, or any defect of spontaneity or plasticity. An element of creation may also be found in arbitrariness, in extrinsic construction, and so forth: but if this element is scanty, one is entitled to say that there is no creation. For there to be creation in a specific sense, and particularly with reference to art, there must be a profound renewal of the past in the intrinsic *possibility*, actually experienced, of an original causality, and, as it were, a sense of glory in this necessity–possibility, which is personal and infinitely impersonal at the same time.

It will be necessary here to return, at the price of repetition, to the concept of the ontological new and its immediate implications.

The problem of the ontological new may be reduced to the problem of an intimate, active power-to-be in its not entirely derived — and not fortuitous — quintessence. This power is, intelligibly, *potentiality* as a reality actually experienced, an inner, intensive, undivided infinite; oneness, individuality; original causality and a value of infinite possibility, of relative impersonality, tranquil and serene greatness that seems to reflect, for example in a painting, the supreme intrinsicality of the cause.

Art draws us close to the secret of an intimate, active power-to-be that carries its cause within, and is therefore felt as infinitely possible and probable. And that, more generally than in the ordinary view, expresses an intimate and ultimate reality: simplicity, purity, freshness of origin, youth without old age.

From a practical viewpoint, the past "makes the present," but from a less approximate and more essential point of view, we must say something quite different: the present is a positivity–creativity that no past can give. Creativity is not transmitted, if it is to be creativity. The original new, as long as it is, is a continuous new, a continuous original light of presence, a continuous original reality of presence. And in this fleeting reality, the values of the spirit are ever newly, originally contained. The physiological and physical conditions, and the surroundings, past and present, contribute to the differentiation and enrichment of these values, but the first cause is in a present creativity, in a centrality or node of values implicit in being as potentiality actually experienced.

Potentiality as actual reality presents a twofold inner infinite: the infinite of an intimate exigency fundamentally incompatible with measure, that is, with its objectively given and measurable being; and, on the other hand, the infinite of its profound intrinsicality of nature, always original — felt as an unlimited possibility and likelihood and as a value of universality. But it must also be said that both the one and the other infinite tend to identify with each other, since the first — the creative new — brings within it, now more, now less, the value and the force of its powerful intrinsicality of nature, that is, of its intimate truth.

Potentiality, as reality actually experienced, is by its own nature an undivided and indivisible moment, one that cannot be divided into parts. It is not properly a *synthesis* (of parts), but is radical, ultimate, original unity in multiplicity. It is the only key that renders intelligible to us a moment of psychic unity, or of any unity whatever that is not merely supposed.

Potentiality — I always mean potentiality as actually experienced reality, indeterminacy, intimate positivity in the making — is inseparable from an implicit negative possibility. Without a negative possibility there would not be what we may call psychic 'dimension' or amplitude, any essentially and powerfully undivided *presence*, a nonmechanical certainty; we would have only a dead reality. Potentiality (implying a negative possibility) is essential in any moment of subjectivity. But what would we say if the negative possibility were held absolutely in abeyance? I reply that one thing is a de facto absolutely excluded alternative, another is a negative possibility altogether consubstantial with possibility itself, absolutely intrinsic in activity inasmuch as it is *activity*.

The inner intensive dynamic infinite is the soul of potentiality as actually experienced reality. The subjective, intensive infinite, which abhors being resolved into given, numerable existents, must nonetheless be conceived, I maintain, as *substance*.

Substance as ultimate reality is conceived in several ways: (1) as unchanging extratemporal reality; (2) as what remains constant throughout all changes; (3) as what sustains itself; and (4) there are those who, in physics, tend to eliminate the notion of substance and to replace it with the sum of the properties that constitute (and exhaust) the object.

By substance I mean that which sustains itself. We cannot, I maintain, conceive of 'ideas' as extratemporal (or atemporal) reality. We cannot turn their powerful, essentially original intrinsic nature into extratemporal static entities that would be absolutely heterogeneous with respect to the genuine value they are supposed to explain. We must substitute for the chiefly practical–utilitarian values of stability and permanence, and immobility and immutability, the value of supreme intrinsicality–authenticity of characterization peculiar to creativity itself.

The intensive inner infinite is *substance* inasmuch as it is essentially — creatively — undivided. It is not reducible to a relation of conditionality. It is felt as a profoundly vital *quid* — a genuine, naked reality, *true by its own strength*, that any predetermination and objectification would exclude. The term 'infinite' (subjective) describes an original creative force better than the term 'indeterminate' (or 'indeterminacy').

We know the actual inner infinite intimately, though often only implicitly, in any reality of thought or of the psyche. Also, the *finite*, as a reality of thought, is an infinite possibility of itself, a *principle of interpretation*. Every line, every point, inasmuch as it is a reality of thought (I mean, of the psyche in general), is subjectivity, unity, undivided presence, active potentiality, an active indeterminate–infinite. This *infinite of identity* is everywhere, now more, now less intensely, where there is subjectivity (potentiality in act, inner transparency, self-awareness; in a certain sense, form).

It is a preeminent characteristic of art to vindicate quality as real. The abstract intellect is inclined to consider reality as, in the last instance, quantitative; to reduce quality to quantity — and to dispose of it as a problem. But in art, quality wants to actuate itself precisely as substance, as a reality that is not simply instrumental, or derivative, or the mere condition of something else. The backbone of art is the quality that is in itself real. Art saves us from being endlessly sent back to an existentiality only inferentially conceived. The same, certainly, could be said of salient moments of practical–ethical activity; but in art this is true in an essentially cognitive–contemplative sphere.

Art has its light and strength, first of all, in the discovery of values ever more central and of infinite opening: discovery or, more truly, creation–revelation, of a harmonious world of essences. Now these *essences* are indeed qualities, concrete concepts, not generalizations and constructions (or schemata, categories, symbols, etc.): they are qualities radically, immediately intrinsic in the subjective, active new.

What we intimately know in the ultimate instance is psychic substance, be it even through the stimulus. The practical mentality tends to stop at the stimulus, at things — whether because they are a given reality, on which one can rely, or because of ignorance — and to despise imagination, including fancy in its varied meanings. Now, to appreciate a work of art, it is important not to ignore the fact that imagination has a profound foundation in the ever-original intrinsic characterization of the creative new, inasmuch as it is immediately in itself creative. Its fleetingness does not exclude a formidable originality–intrinsicality of nature.

It is altogether wrong to contrast pictorial vision with, essentially, a first, elementary sensation, also called 'retinal' or 'ocular.' And this not only because there is no sensation (as discovered by psychologists in repeated, refined experiments) that does not reflect expectations, fears, hopes, and other anticipations, but much more radically, absolutely, because any sensation is already subjectivity, with what it implies.

A beautiful painting shows us in every brushstroke the immediate spirituality of sensation. Sensation is not used therein as a *means*. Equally, there is nothing in it that is properly an object: sensation is in itself an active subject, even if, in certain respects and with some reservations, it may be called 'object.' Everything is soul, intrinsicality–authenticity (auto-creativity). Hence the value of immediacy of painting. In an inferior painting, however, sensation tends to be *used*, and it is not profoundly identified with the true active subject, it is not spirit: it is nothing that may recall to us the integrity and concreteness of the Logos — that is, of an uncaused causality (in itself causal). For it is here that one sees great art: when sensation itself is spirit.

Any first sensation is already a spatial opening, as subjective reality; it is already reality of inner transparency and unity and presence. The lightness of touch is already the indeterminate–infinite proper to the *finite* inasmuch as it is sensation or perception, that is, inasmuch as it is reality of thought (psychical), against the inertia, the insignificance, the heaviness, the finiteness of abstract matter. Art lets us discover—it is understood, in our own thought—a delicate positivity of reality that is not grasped by the abstract intellect and that is not reached through successive extensions. And there is no reason why this secret of freshness, of lightness, and of limpidity — of simplicity, of chastity, of virginity, of silence — should not be latent in the most fleeting glimmer of color-light.

It is also one of the first steps of a gross and naive derivationism to conceive of sensation as a first, almost insignificant element that presents no problems, starting from which it may be possible to explain actual reality in its superior forms: a derivationism with which we deceive ourselves into thinking we can reach the solution to any problem.

But then why the slight significance of any ordinary perception, for instance, of a noise? Would life perhaps become intolerable if every sensation raised itself in song? Or because any sensation used as an instrument would be ipso facto impaired? Obviously these explanations are not satisfactory. We may rather conjecture that there is a sort of bifurcation in biological processes, so that on the one hand sensation — or sensibility — is ever renewed according to its fundamental character, that is, as a principle of subjectivity; and on the other hand it organizes and limits itself in its competence and is made strictly dependent on determined organs of determined functions. But, in my view, its primary and fundamental nature nonetheless remains that which makes sensation into one reality with the principle of subjectivity itself, a qualitative force that belongs essentially to creative thought, and from time to time beckons, so to speak, even in sensibility restricted to functions of usefulness and practical necessity.

It harms the indeterminist thesis to conceive indeterminacy as properly defined by the power of *choice*. Being as an active power-to-be defines indeterminacy, but only if it is intended as a force–exigency itself constitutive of being, as a reality identically final and causal in itself, as a motive-value that gets its quality and its force from being essentially not-given, and not properly as a choice. *Choice* presupposes an objectification of the problem involved, a determined extrinsic end, which brings us back, or tends to bring us back, into extrinsic causality–finality — the negation of the interior infinite of potentiality in act. There are generally in choice a pre-existent subject that chooses; objectified and given motives; pro-cesses of extrinsic causality and formal necessity; hypothetically, an absolute chance, not necessarily indeterminacy. Indeterminacy is, rather, vocation: the moment of a dynamic indeterminate–infinite, to which it is vital and constitutive to refuse any absolutely pre-determined measure of itself. We must not look for indeterminacy in the *arbitrium indifferentiae*, but in the heart of the positivity of subjective being, in a profound spontaneity that contrasts both with mechanism and with abstract will.

The indeterminacy we are dealing with does not consist pri-marily of a yes or a no, much less in a newness of mere change, but in a newness of reality, an ontological newness of origin, of crea-tivity, in itself purposive and causal — that may be very similar to the preceding moment, but is *positivity* of such reality that it is not transmitted or inherited, or communicated through force of inertia, and is always an original producing. Such creative quintessence is characterized and intimately constituted by the very fact of its origi-nally creating itself: a nucleus of immediate implications, not a game in a childish plot, but an immense reality.

We must not, however, forget that ordinarily, in our everyday life, we find before us an activity that is not at all creativity to an eminent degree, and in contrast with which creativity itself assumes more than ever its distinct significance. This is the case if it is aphoristically said that we "learn a technique, not art"; or when we say that, to our judgment, a certain work of art is inferior to another because "there is more will than sensitivity." And yet essentially the same dynamic inner indeterminate–infinite is found, as I hold, in creative imagination, in will, in decision, in effort, and sometimes to more than a slight degree! How do we explain such diverse appearance and value? We may reply that in will, in effort, in analytic attention, etc., the extrinsic action actuates itself as a force altogether directed outward and set on concentrating itself in order to act efficiently, to the detriment of all qualitative–cognitive content proper to it and of all intimate, immediate sensuous plasticity. Furthermore, in art — in creative spontaneity and in sensibility — something originally luminous beckons, while in effort, in decision, in initiative, we do not notice such a source, perhaps because it is too familiar and close to us. In spontaneity and creativity the same source reveals to us its overpowering intrinsicality of nature, in which we identify ourselves and that at the same time overshadows us. Spontaneity and sensibility (more than will, even though directed to a cognitive end) let us know, or glimpse, the virginity and germinal richness of that original node of which I speak — and that many prefer to ignore.

Spontaneity implies that representation is not an object, but a subject–agent. Properly the artist does not seek: he is called by that inner intensive infinite that is the ultimate substance of quality. The more objectified, constructed, thought is, and also the more it is explicit, the more it risks being poor and unilateral. Thus it is not rare that the greatest poets are unrecognizable when they write in prose. Because poetry is, before anything else, the substance of truth in the creative new; because there is this creative essence, this nucleus of truths inherent in a creative new, that we are slow to recognize. The soul of song encloses and discloses an immense mystery, something autogenous, in itself purposive and causal, fertile with ever-new truths.

The passage from intrinsic to extrinsic causality is only gradual. The prevailing of something strictly deliberate in the activity of thought indicates the loss of spontaneity: indicates the passage of what is creative to what is externally constructive, schematic, dogmatic, abstract, one sided — and from the authentic work of art to the offensive one. Profound spontaneity, opposed to what is schematic, formal, and forced, means intimate truth because it means creativity, presence of values intimately related to the original new, spiritual concreteness, value of comprehension not deliberately limited. It expresses something naked, genuine, authentic, ultimate, in itself causal, intimately true — all values that confirm the concept of the non-arbitrariness of the Logos, as the concept of a nucleus of values inherent in the original new.

Many times art theorists themselves promiscuously use the terms 'creation' and 'construction' — revealing a gap that is reflected in all their work. Properly creation should develop *ab intrinseco*, with an ever-new realizing, in their reciprocal implications, of values germinally inherent in the creative new. This harmony *ab intrinseco, ex novo*, places an abyss between creation and construction (in an exterior sense). It is well understood, however, that even in construction, based as it is on given elements, as long as we do not fall into pure mechanism we shall have to admit an element of creation, however slight.

Often the kinships in an ever-original causality spring into our minds ready-formed, felicitously expressed, sudden. The inner workings of the subconscious (whatever it is) in, as we may conjecture, an extremely docile and ready element, amaze us. Nevertheless, spontaneity does not draw its value and reality particularly from the subliminal. The activity in the fertile secret workshop must be immense but does not essentially constitute the proper value of spontaneity. Indeed, the reality of the latter rests in an original and profound intrinsicality of nature that belongs to all psychic activity. The terms 'spontaneity,' 'freedom,' 'responsibility,' 'creativity,' 'intimate reality–truth,' all the terms or concepts implying in the first place the idea of an intensive indeterminate–infinite as a source of value and activity, belong equally to the subliminal and the ordinary consciousness, and to the practical spirit and the poetic–cognitive one. For instance, our very faith in the value of being as in something that may but must not be lacking seems to imply a certain earnestness, a certain sense of responsibility, also and all the more in poetic discourse — unless 'responsibility' is understood in a very restricted and superficial sense.

The problem of spontaneity touches closely so-called abstract art. We know that external reality, the so-called 'subject,' is not much more than an opportunity for expressing essential inner motive–values. Abstractionism, however, by deliberately excluding external and figurative reality, and by purposely seeking intimate, original value, risks a lesser spontaneity, particularly in two respects:

1. The exigency of omni-comprehension, of non-unilaterality, of integrity and real knowledge in the spirit — in itself a supreme motive-value and original force of thought — weakens with the *deliberate* exclusion of a part of reality, and this to the detriment, in the plastic arts, of a freer and more profound spontaneity.

2. The intimate essential values themselves, when directly sought, are easily reduced to objects, to determined ends, and, being objectified, are no longer the same. The painter who seeks, for example, simplicity, intimacy, unity, freshness, a sense of intimate authenticity–universality or other intrinsic motive-values of the activity of thought risks objectifying them and losing them, risks falling into arbitrariness, into *constructed* reality, into the unilateral, into a spiritual void. The melodious intention kills the song. Genuine lyricalness, on the contrary, almost unconsciously, involuntarily, and immediately, qualifies the object, in which it enriches and reveals itself and through which it gains power.

But it is not permissible to dictate: the power of thought is such that we cannot exclude the possibility that it may find anew its vertiginous reality of present origin despite any kind of objectification, or mummification, or program, or school, or theory.

Accustomed as we are to holding as a well established fact that energy, as it is said, can neither be created nor destroyed, it becomes all the more difficult to admit indeterminacy. For the negation of a creation of force or energy is the negation of indeterminism (unless 'indeterminacy' is understood as absolute chance).

Today's physical science shows that determinism in physics is not demonstrated. As for the idea that the creation of force or energy is inadmissible, it may be said that it is no longer dogma. On the contrary, the progressive leveling of energy through infinite time seems to force us to postulate as a counteraction a creation of energy.

Physics, especially the general theory of relativity, tends to banish the very concept of force, while reducing it to a property of space–time. And we must take refuge in our intimate experience of a force — or power — essentially qualitative, that sustains itself, that is to say, renews itself, positively, that is to say creatively, not by force of inertia.

In the history of philosophy and science, save for rare and doubtful exceptions, we find that, generally, even when the theme is creative force and not force of inertia, force is represented as an impulse given once and for all: the problem of an *actual* positivity of intimate force hardly arises, if I am not mistaken, in an explicit way, and it seems that we always fall back on the concept of a conservation of energy or force that means inertia — the conservation or equilibrium of the quantity of movement.

I speak of qualitative force because quality — particularly in art — is a motive-value: it is indistinguishably a plastic force. There is no value without intrinsic force, born with and from value itself. The concept of force is not born — or is not only born, as others would want it to be — from muscular sensations, but from the conviction of an intimate causality, from will and power themselves (intimate, active). This force, primordial and not of inertia, is what is most familiar to us. Are we sure not to err if in order to explain it we try to reduce it to something else? Why do we not consider that if we neglect this present active potentiality there is perhaps nothing left that we know intimately as reality?

Obviously the term 'force' brings us to the world of violence, and extrinsic causality, and material execution. But we also say 'force of vision,' 'force of thought,' and so on, and force is similarly implicit in intrinsic causality, in the most generous senses of charity and love. The terms 'force' and 'power' are often interchangeable, but the term 'power' has in certain respects a broader meaning, while 'force' refers more particularly to physical causality and is also conceived altogether as a function of mass and movement.

There are those who, with respect to the value of a work of art, like to point out the power of its represented movements to communicate energy. Truly, there are too many no less efficient methods of exciting energy. The contemplative spirit will recognize and find itself with greater ease in the silence and apparent immobility of the creation. But I want to stress that this immobility is not static, it is not the conservation of inert matter; on the contrary — like the actual infinite of love — it is the expression of creativity in its intrinsic or 'eternal' (not extra- or supertemporal) character, supreme *force* and ever-new reality.

Here, against indeterminism, will recur the argument of sufficient reason. It will be opposed: "How will force create itself if, before, it is not?" There is no doubt: the necessity of an antecedent, once admitted, ultimately excludes any origin or creation. And I have no other answer than this one: our logic must get used to the idea of a being that, insofar as it *is*, is identically and immediately creativity with regard to itself.

In contact with matter, thought (mental or psychic reality), if we admit that it is not an illusion, should lose — and yet not lose — the intensive indeterminate–infinite that is the heart of active potentiality; it should be a *thing*, not a thought any longer, nor any more a reality of inner transparency and undivided presence: it should be reduced — and yet not be reduced! — to something inert, dead. Or otherwise how could it have any efficacious relation, active or passive, to matter itself?* The difficulty certainly exists, so much so that to solve or elude it some have denied matter and some have denied subjectivity. But good sense, generally, yields to the everyday experiencing of an efficacious relation between the psychic and the physical or physiological.

In the plastic arts one discovers with special evidence a power

* Cf. chapter 3 of this volume.

that is at one and the same time intelligent and dynamic (plastic). The painter, or the sculptor, will ever be immersed in the living — though only implicit — consciousness of a concreated corporeity of his own sensitivity, which the contact, whatever it is, with matter does not contradict or destroy, but rather enriches and intensifies. The same should be said regarding any order of activity, but in art the close and fecund relationship between quality and the material means presents a problem especially alive and near.

It seems that this element of exteriority–resistance should be held as coessential with the *new* — that is, with the positivity of subjective being — with no less right than its other aspects that are more intimately and more clearly intelligible.

No aesthetic is possible without the study of the profoundly intrinsic nature of an original or creative principle. Critics and philosophers struggle between rigid regularity and, on the other hand, what is called 'subjective' in a pejorative sense; and they look for a compromise, a halfway measure. And they ignore another and stronger reality, that is, a node of origin that carries within itself, indissolubly, novelty and constancy, a constancy born of the most intimate and jealous nature of the new.

CHAPTER 7

The Principle of Indeterminacy
and the Subjective Infinite

To try to understand the nature of indeterminism we must study the nature of the Infinite and consider its various meanings:

1. There is the indeterminate–infinite of subatomic physics, which shows only that a rigorous determinism has not been demonstrated, and, in any case, could probably not be achieved. Here we do not see indeterminacy as intimate value and reality.

2. There is the objective indeterminate–infinite, as when we talk of the infinity of space, of time, of the stars, of drops of water in the sea, of grains of sand. The objective infinite does not constitute a value in itself, but it can represent an incentive, an opportunity, a medium of expression for the intimate–infinite and for a value of originality.

3. Altogether different is the intensive indeterminate–infinite, that is, the infinite of identity (i.e., the inner, substantial, dynamic, subjective, intimate infinite). This is profoundly immanent in psychic reality, or, better still, is all one with it. For example, the

terms 'potentiality' (actually experienced), 'unicity,' 'undivided,' 'identity of self with self,' 'unity,' 'value of universality,' 'inner necessity,' 'intrinsicality of nature,' 'eternal' (not in the sense of super- or extratemporal), 'intrinsic,' etc., equally describe or imply either subjectivity or an absolutely inherent active infinite.

'Potentiality,' as actually experienced reality, can indeed be another term for the principle of indeterminacy. A still better term, I would say, is 'infinite': inner, subjective, dynamic, creative, qualitative infinite; infinite of identity, of intensity, of freedom — irreplaceable, vitally and essentially nonobjectifiable, immeasurable.

Because it lacks form, it may seem that we should deny the inner infinite its reality — other than a reality of appearance or as 'epiphenomenon.' Form has twofold reality: *eternal birth* and *abstract conservation.* (In other words, plastic, creative, formative, active form; and on the other hand, shaped, finite, static, limited, material form.) Actually, the two aspects do not exclude one another at all. In form the *given*, the finite, must also ever be *not given, a great expectancy*: here is the secret of its delicacy, its transparency and its unity and value. It is, as it were, an inner contrast, this which gives life to form. The infinite of identity is, for instance, to be found in ecstasy, in love (questi, che mai da me non fia diviso . . .),* in contemplation, in any presence (inasmuch as it is psychic reality). It is also found, though indirectly, in the idea of usefulness, of conditionality and functionality, in fanaticism and idolatry, and in avarice. But it is a supreme error to confuse the static immutable (inert, immobile, totally passive) with the intrinsic, active–immutable, the self-sustaining infinite of identity.

* "He, who shall never be divided from me . . . ." *Inferno,* 5. 135.

We know, or believe we know, that this quality of indeterminate–infinite that belongs to the essence of subjectivity and the psyche cannot truly be substance in the philosophic sense unless there is inherent in it an element of exteriority, of resistance; but is this sufficient to condemn it as an illusion or an epiphenomenon? The static, passive, instrumental object is a *condition* of being and of becoming, but it is also the most remote from the spirit of life. No joining or interpenetration of parts can achieve the miracle of a true, ultimate unity of substance; it needs the dynamic power that we feel actualizing itself as an originally undivided whole, without discontinuity, in the subjective being intended as actual, living power-to-be.

We must admit as dynamic reality, even though hypothetically, an intimate power-to-be. It isn't clear that this *infinite of identity* — the psyche's own, the actual indeterminate–infinite — may not reach such a point of concentration (of resistance, measurability, objectivity, hardness) as to have plastic efficacy, that is, a direct relationship with the physical, *without losing its own nature*. Contemporary physics admits, even though in a provisional way, many other exceptions to ordinary logic (cf. the duality wave-corpuscle) and invites to greater perplexities in other fields as well.

Why, at times, the great abyss of death, when according to all common sense death ought to be desirable to us? If it is an instinct, what is this instinct? Why such a deep repugnance? This abyss perhaps reflects the boundless vastness that belongs to the very intrinsic nature of any moment, however fleeting. It reflects the powerful *intrinsicality of nature* of this inner infinite — which is lost if it is objectified and measured and made into a finite thing, and which we wrongly do not study more assiduously.

In ancient times, in philosophy the fundamental reality was the *finite*: whether what was in question were *things* or ideas — immobile ideas, immutable either because preserving themselves as such, or because already perfect. In medieval times the idea of extrinsic causality, including strict will, was perhaps in the foreground. In more recent times, there has tended to emerge the reality of a becoming: creativity, time, the positivity of being, being as an original causality, value, and substance in itself, the problem of that which is *originally* self-sustaining, *causa sui*, an immanent cause, an eternal birth.

Without the indeterminate–infinite of the subjective being we lose the subjectivity of activity; we fall into a world that is absolutely inertial, without original causality, divisible, numerical, discontinuous, derivative. We ban the *causa sui*. We deem intrinsic causality illogical, and we don't ask ourselves whether the negation of any true pulse of life isn't absurd, unless we hold that we simply have to do with chance, or otherwise with something decidedly transcendent.

But the study of an original causality has the merit of lending itself to being deepened. The intensive infinite of indeterminacy is perhaps the most essential thing of dynamic (actual, subjective, present, not given or measurable, not static, not discontinuous or dead) *being*. We have to consider illogical the *causa sui* if we start from the dogma '*Nihil ex nihilo*' if we don't admit reality in what is self-sustaining, if everything must be reducible to something else, if everything must be inert, in a world of total inertia.

The intensive, actual psychodynamic ability-to-be is at least something about which we have a beginning of knowledge. It is reality and value of amplitude, virginity, light, unicity, possibility, individuality, universality and intrinsic necessity, verisimilitude, spiritual integrity, intimate and profound and delicate touch. Thus it is, for example, that *virginity* and *infinite* (subjective) have a profound and revealing kinship in the immediate value of creativity, which is an immense thing.

Additional parallel chains of causal processes will lead to analogous results. But in these chains of strict conditionality other real, constitutive causes occur that are intrinsically characterized and not of an absolutely derivative or passively repetitive nature. The sense of a common nature makes us think of an originally constant, yet always new and independent, force of subjectivity in its successive moments: *constant because creative.*

Philosophy in us begins with our sensitivity to this core of original unity–identity. But to pretend to explain such an awesome intrinsicality of characterization of the subjective being by denying or ignoring the reality of time is a false and desperate undertaking.

CHAPTER 8

Time and the Positivity of Being

Time is the very positivity of being. Time cannot be abolished, nor can it be reduced to a mere succession of reversible phenomena without doing away with creativity and every profound motive quality and reality of origin.

Poetry shows us a relationship between silence and love.* The same may be said of art in general when it attains a *virginity* that is ultimate essence. This may be expressed equally well by the term 'potentiality' (value of potentiality actually experienced), and by 'indeterminacy' and 'creativity,' and this is a formidable intrinsicality of the nature of being.

Psychic unity — the undivided, inner transparency, the psychic present, multiplicity–unity — lives only as potentiality (actually experienced), as the moment, as time.

The urge-to-be is one with being: it is not an antecedent.

One is inasmuch as one is *originally*: not because or inasmuch

* See, e.g., Shelley, *Hymn of Pan*, v. 23: "And all that did then attend and follow, / Were silent with love . . . ."

[135]

as one derives from another. The ultimate substance of not-being will never be found.

Being is an immediate and continuous tension against not being. Positivity of being (time) is positivity as long as it is identically *possibility*, that is, as long as it checks and keeps in abeyance a negative possibility. It is the abyss of death that makes life great.

The essence of being is an original necessity to be (an immediate, immanent, native *necessity-to-be*).

The subjective, intensive infinite is creativity itself, the measureless freedom of creativity. It is, I think, the impression of living at an irreplaceable level of light — irreplaceable in its ultimate spontaneity, or genuineness, or native freshness.

The subjective infinite is value because it is the irreplaceable source, the true origin; it contains the miracle (mystery, secret, problem) of reality and being. We certainly miss the mark if we presume to strip it of all reality or reduce it to an illusion by calling it simply 'subjective' ...

Every psychic moment is a *presence*: it is an infinite of identity.

One or more inert things are not and do not constitute a *presence*.

Time is the essence of the spirit. It is the very urge to include in the same sweep both the given and the infinitely possible: it is a moment of newness and of responsibility; it is a moment of acute pain, remorse, regret, desperation, hope.

The principle of indeterminacy is one with potentiality (as actual, actually experienced reality); it is one with the subjective infinite (as its own presence in itself, reality in itself, subjectivity); one with irreversibility (as reality, value, force of irreversibility, of noninertia) and with positivity of being, as opposed to mere existing (static, dead, objectified, immobile, quantitative, numerable ...).

I remain ever more convinced that the subjective infinite is the ultimate substance, that it is one with indeterminacy meant as actual reality of origin. The assiduous study of precognitive phenomena demonstrates that we are involved in a net of anticipations and multiplications, but it does not demonstrate that time (indeterminacy, irreversibility) is rigorously canceled. For this to be a fact we would have to witness extremely detailed prophecies, millennia or at least centuries before what is prophesied happens; but these do not occur.

Architecture can give us inertia (conservation, utility, functionality), and at the same time ecstasy, as a value of eternal birth, an eternal origin, an eternal problem. There is in the numberless forms of every field of activity a deep problematical quality or potentiality actually experienced, and there are, on the other hand, rigidly related links of extrinsic conditionality. There is, or there may be, an aura of freshness, almost an anxious grace, accompanying the numberless forms, anticipating them, directing them, tending to forerun them, to precede rather than follow them.

Will not he who denies inner causality reduce everything to a state of inertia?

Art is the revelation of an original causality: of a *virginity* of being. The study of the subjective, intensive *infinite* as a positive ultimate reality seems to lead us closer to something that is self-sustaining. And it leads us away from the profound incomprehensibility of quantum physics and other relatively valid doctrines.